ANCIENT ROME
BEEKEEPING

PLINY ~ COLUMELLA ~ VARRO ~ VIRGIL

CONTENTS

CHAPTER I

BEES IN PLINY'S

NATURAL HISTORY

―――――――――

Among all insects, the first rank, and our especial admiration, ought, in justice, to be accorded to bees, which alone, of all the insects, have been created for the benefit of man. They extract honey and collect it, a juicy substance remarkable for its extreme sweetness, lightness, and wholesomeness. They form their combs and collect wax, an article that is useful for a thousand purposes of life; they are patient of fatigue, toil at their labours, form themselves into political communities, hold councils together in private, elect chiefs in common, and, a thing that is the most remarkable of all, have their own code of morals. In addition to this, being as they are, neither tame nor wild, so all-powerful is Nature, that, from a creature so minute as to be nothing more hardly than the shadow of an animal, she has created a marvel beyond all comparison. What muscular power, what exertion of strength are we to put in comparison with such vast energy and such industry as theirs? What display of human genius, in a word, shall we compare with the reasoning powers manifested by them? In this they have, at all events, the advantage of us — they know of nothing but what is for the common benefit of all. Away, then, with all questions whether they respire or no, and let us be ready to agree on the question of their blood; and yet, how little of it can possibly exist in bodies so minute as theirs. — And now let us form some idea of the instinct they display.

Bees keep within the hive during the winter — for whence are they to derive the strength requisite to withstand frosts and snows, and the northern blasts? The same, in fact, is done by all insects, but not to so late a period; as those which conceal themselves in the walls of our houses, are much sooner sensible of the returning warmth. With reference to bees, either seasons and climates have considerably changed, or else former writers have been greatly mistaken. They retire for the winter at the setting of the Vergiliæ, and remain shut up till after the rising of that constellation, and not till only the beginning of spring, as some authors have stated; nor, indeed, does any one in Italy ever think of then opening the hives. They do not come forth to ply their labours until the bean blossoms; and then not a day do they lose in inactivity, while the weather is favourable for their pursuits.

First of all, they set about constructing their combs, and forming the wax, or, in other words, making their dwellings and cells; after this they produce their young, and then make honey and wax from flowers, and extract bee-glue from the tears of those trees which distil glutinous substances, the juices, gums, and resins, namely, of the willow, the elm, and the reed. With these substances, as well as others of a more bitter nature, they first line the whole inside of the hive, as a sort of protection against the greedy propensities of other small insects, as they are well aware that they are about to form that which will prove an object of attraction to them. Having done this, they employ similar substances in narrowing the entrance to the hive, if otherwise too wide.

The persons who understand this subject, call the substance which forms the first foundation of their combs, commosis, the next, pissoceros, and the third propolis; which last is placed between the other layers and the wax, and is remarkable for its utility in medicine. The commosis forms the first crust or layer, and has a bitter taste; and upon it is laid the pissoceros, a kind of thin wax, which acts as a sort of varnish. The propolis is produced from the sweet gum of the vine or the poplar, and is of a denser consistency, the juices of flowers being added to it. Still, however, it cannot be properly termed wax, but rather the foundation of the honey-combs; by means of it all inlets are stopped up, which might, otherwise, serve for the admission of cold or other injurious influences; it has also a strong odour, so much so, indeed, that many people use it instead of galbanum.

In addition to this, the bees form collections of erithace or bee-bread, which some persons call "sandaraca," and others "cerinthos." This is to serve as the food of the bees while they are at work, and is often found stowed away in the cavities of the cells, being of a bitter flavour also. It is produced from the spring dews and the gummy juices of trees, being less abundant while the south-west wind is blowing, and blackened by the prevalence of a south wind. On the other hand, again, it is of a reddish colour and becomes improved by the north-east wind; it is found in the greatest abundance upon the nut trees in Greece. Menecrates says, that it is a flower, which gives indications of the nature of the coming harvest; but no one says so, with the exception of him.

Bees form wax from the blossoms of all trees and plants, with the sole exception of the rumex and the echinopodes, both being kinds of herbs. It is by mistake, however, that spartum is excepted; for many varieties of honey that come from Spain, and have been made in the plantations of it, have a strong taste of that plant. I am of opinion, also, that it is without any sufficient reason that the olive has been excepted, seeing that it is a well-known fact, that where olives are in the greatest abundance, the swarms of bees are the most numerous. Bees are not injurious to fruit of any kind; they will never settle on a dead flower, much less a dead carcase. They pursue their labours within three-score paces of their hives; and when the flowers in their vicinity are exhausted, they send out scouts from time to time, to discover places for forage at a greater distance. When overtaken by night in their expeditions, they watch till the morning, lying on their backs, in order to protect their wings from the action of the dew.

It is not surprising that there have been persons who have made bees their exclusive study; Aristomachus of Soli, for instance, who for a period of fifty-eight years did nothing else; Philiscus of Thasos, also, surnamed Agrius, who passed his life in desert spots, tending swarms of bees. Both of these have written works on this subject.

The manner in which bees carry on their work is as follows. In the day time a guard is stationed at the entrance of the hive, like the sentries in a camp. At night they take their rest until the morning, when one of them awakes the rest with a humming noise, repeated twice or thrice, just as though it were sounding a trumpet. They then take their flight in a body, if the day is likely to turn out fine; for they have the gift of foreknowing wind and rain, and in such case will keep close within their dwellings. On the other hand, when the weather is fine — and this, too, they have the power of foreknowing — the swarm issues forth, and at once applies itself to its work, some loading their legs from the flowers, while others fill their mouths with water, and charge the downy surface of their bodies with drops of liquid. Those among them that are young go forth to their labours, and collect the materials already mentioned, while those that are more aged stay within the hives and work. The bees whose business it is to carry the flowers, with their fore feet load their thighs, which Nature has made rough for the purpose, and with their trunks load their fore feet: bending beneath their load, they then return to the hive, where there are three or four bees ready to receive them, and aid in discharging their burdens. For, within the hive as well, they have their allotted duties to perform: some are engaged in building, others in smoothing, the combs, while others again are occupied in passing on the materials, and others in preparing food from the provision which has been brought; that there may be no unequal division, either in their labour, their food, or the distribution of their time, they do not even feed separately.

Commencing at the vaulted roof of the hive, they begin the construction of their cells, and, just as we do in the manufacture of a web, they construct their cells from top to bottom, taking care to leave two passages around each compartment, for the entrance of some and the exit of others. The combs, which are fastened to the hive in the upper part, and in a slight degree also at the sides, adhere to each other, and are thus suspended altogether. They do not touch the floor of the hive, and are either angular or round, according to its shape; sometimes, in fact, they are both angular and round at once, when two swarms are living in unison, but have dissimilar modes of operation. They prop up the combs that are likely to fall, by means of arched pillars, at intervals springing from the floor, so as to leave them a passage for the purpose of effecting repairs. The first three ranks of their cells are generally left empty when constructed, that there may be nothing exposed to view which may invite theft; and it is the last ones, more especially, that are filled with honey: hence it is that the combs are always taken out at the back of the hive.

The bees that are employed in carrying look out for a favourable breeze, and if a gale should happen to spring up, they poise themselves in the air with little stones, by way of ballast; some writers, indeed, say that they place them upon their shoulders. When the wind is contrary, they fly close to the ground, taking care, however, to keep clear of the brambles. It is wonderful what strict watch is kept upon their work: all instances of idleness are carefully remarked, the offenders are chastised, and on a repetition of the fault, punished with death. Their sense of cleanliness, too, is quite extraordinary; everything is removed that might be in the way, and no filth is allowed to remain in the midst of their work. The ordure even of those that are at work within, that they may not have to retire to any distance, is all collected in one spot, and on stormy days, when they are obliged to cease their ordinary labours, they employ themselves in carrying it out. When it grows towards evening, the buzzing in the hive becomes gradually less and less, until at last one of their number is to be seen flying about the hive with the same loud humming noise with which they were aroused in the morning, thereby giving the signal, as it were, to retire to rest: in this, too, they imitate the usage of the camp. The moment the signal is heard, all is silent.

They first construct the dwellings of the commonalty, and then those of the king-bee. If they have reason to expect an abundant season, they add abodes also for the drones: these are cells of a smaller size, though the drones themselves are larger than the bees.

The drones have no sting, and would seem to be a kind of imperfect bee, formed the very last of all; the expiring effort, as it were, of worn-out and exhausted old age, a late and tardy offspring, and doomed, in a measure, to be the slaves of the genuine bees. Hence it is that the bees exercise over them a rigorous authority, compel them to take the foremost rank in their labours, and if they show any sluggishness, punish them without mercy. And not only in their labours do the drones give them their assistance, but in the propagation of their species as well, the very multitude of them contributing greatly to the warmth of the hive. At all events, it is a well-known fact, that the greater the multitude of the drones, the more numerous is sure to be the progeny of the swarm. When the honey is beginning to come to maturity, the bees drive away the drones, and setting upon each in great numbers, put them all to death. It is only in the spring that the drones are ever to be seen. If you deprive a drone of its wings, and then replace it in the hive, it will pull off the wings of the other drones.

HONEY

In the lower part of the hive they construct for their future sovereign a palatial abode, spacious and grand, separated from the rest, and surmounted by a sort of dome: if this prominence should happen to be flattened, all hopes of progeny are lost. All the cells are hexagonal, each foot having formed its own side. No part of this work, however, is done at any stated time, as the bees seize every opportunity for the performance of their task when the days are fine; in one or two days, at most, they fill their cells with honey.

This substance is engendered from the air, mostly at the rising of the constellations, and more especially when Sirius is shining; never, however, before the rising of the Vergiliæ, and then just before day-break. Hence it is, that at early dawn the leaves of the trees are found covered with a kind of honey-like dew, and those who go into the open air at an early hour in the morning, find their clothes covered, and their hair matted, with a sort of unctuous liquid. Whether it is that this liquid is the sweat of the heavens, or whether a saliva emanating from the stars, or a juice exuding from the air while purifying itself, would that it had been, when it comes to us, pure, limpid, and genuine, as it was, when first it took its downward descent. But as it is, falling from so vast a height, attracting corruption in its passage, and tainted by the exhalations of the earth as it meets them, sucked, too, as it is from off the trees and the herbage of the fields, and accumulated in the stomachs of the bees — for they cast it up again through the mouth — deteriorated besides by the juices of flowers, and then steeped within the hives and subjected to such repeated changes — still, in spite of all this, it affords us by its flavour a most exquisite pleasure, the result, no doubt, of its æthereal nature and origin.

The honey is always best in those countries where it is to be found deposited in the calix of the most exquisite flowers, such, for instance, as the districts of Hymettus and Hybla, in Attica and Sicily respectively, and after them the island of Calydna. At first, honey is thin, like water, after which it effervesces for some days, and purifies itself like must. On the twentieth day it begins to thicken, and soon after becomes covered with a thin membrane, which gradually increases through the scum which is thrown up by the heat. The honey of the very finest flavour, and the least tainted by the leaves of trees, is that gathered from the foliage of the oak and the linden, and from reeds.

The peculiar excellence of honey depends, as already stated, on the country in which it is produced; the modes, too, of estimating its quality are numerous. In some countries we find the honey-comb remarkable for the goodness of the wax, as in Sicily, for instance, and the country of the Peligni; in other places the honey itself is found in greater abundance, as in Crete, Cyprus, and Africa; and in others, again, the comb is remarkable for its size; the northern climates, for instance, for in Germany a comb has been known to be as much as eight feet in length, and quite black on the concave surface.

But whatever the country in which it may happen to have been produced, there are three different kinds of honey. — Spring honey is that made in a comb which has been constructed of flowers, from which circumstance it has received the name of anthinum. There are some persons who say that this should not be touched, because the more abundant the nutriment, the stronger will be the coming swarm; while others, again, leave less of this honey than of any other for the bees, on the ground that there is sure to be a vast abundance at the rising of the greater constellations, as well as at the summer solstice, when the thyme and the vine begin to blossom, for then they are sure to find abundant materials for their cells.

In taking the combs the greatest care is always requisite, for when they are stinted for food the bees become desperate, and either pine to death, or else wing their flight to other places: but on the other hand, over-abundance will entail idleness, and then they will feed upon the honey, and not the bee-bread. Hence it is that the most careful breeders take care to leave the bees a fifteenth part of this gathering. There is a certain day for beginning the honey-gathering, fixed, as it were, by a law of Nature, if men would only understand or observe it, being the thirtieth day after the bees have swarmed and come forth. This gathering mostly takes place before the end of May.

The second kind of honey is "summer honey," which, from the circumstance of its being produced at the most favourable season, has received the Greek name of horaion;

it is generally made during the next thirty days after the solstice, while Sirius is shining in all its brilliancy. Nature has revealed in this substance most remarkable properties to mortals, were it not that the fraudulent propensities of man are apt to falsify and corrupt everything. For, after the rising of each constellation, and those of the highest rank more particularly, or after the appearance of the rainbow, if a shower does not ensue, but the dew becomes warmed by the sun's rays, a medicament, and not real honey, is produced; a gift sent from heaven for the cure of diseases of the eyes, ulcers, and maladies of the internal viscera. If this is taken at the rising of Sirius, and the rising of Venus, Jupiter, or Mercury should happen to fall on the same day, as often is the case, the sweetness of this substance, and the virtue which it possesses of restoring men to life, are not inferior to those attributed to the nectar of the gods.

The crop of honey is most abundant if gathered at full moon, and it is richest when the weather is fine. In all honey, that which flows of itself, like must or oil, has received from us the name of acetum. The summer honey is the most esteemed of all, from the fact of its being made when the weather is driest: it is looked upon as the most serviceable when made from thyme; it is then of a golden colour, and of a most delicious flavour. The honey that we see formed in the calix of flowers is of a rich and unctuous nature; that which is made from rosemary is thick, while that which is candied is little esteemed. Thyme honey does not coagulate, and on being touched will draw out into thin viscous threads, a thing which is the principal proof of its heaviness. When honey shows no tenacity, and the drops immediately part from one another, it is looked upon as a sign of its worthlessness. The other proofs of its goodness are the fine aroma of its smell, its being of a sweetness that closely borders on the sour, and being glutinous and pellucid.

Cassius Dionysius is of opinion that in the summer gathering the tenth part of the honey ought to be left for the bees if the hives should happen to be well filled, and even if not, still in the same proportion; while, on the other hand, if there is but little in them, he recommends that it should not be touched at all. The people of Attica have fixed the period for commencing this gathering at the first ripening of the wild fig; others have made it the day that is sacred to Vulcan.

The third kind of honey, which is the least esteemed of all, is the wild honey, known by the name of ericæum. It is collected by the bees after the first showers of autumn, when the heather alone is blooming in the woods, from which circumstance it derives its sandy appearance. It is mostly produced at the rising of Arcturus, beginning at the day before the ides of September. Some persons delay the gathering of the summer honey until the rising of Arcturus, because from then till the autumnal equinox there are fourteen days left, and it is from the equinox till the setting of the Vergiliæ, a period of forty-eight days, that the heather is in the greatest abundance. The Athenians call this plant by the name of tetralix, and the Eubœans sisirum, and they look upon it as affording great pleasure to the bees to browse upon, probably because there are no other flowers for them to resort to. This gathering terminates at the end of the vintage and the setting of the Vergiliæ, mostly about the ides of November. Experience teaches us that we ought to leave for the bees two-thirds of this crop, and always that part of the combs as well, which contains the bee-bread.

From the winter solstice to the rising of Arcturus the bees are buried in sleep for sixty days, and live without any nourishment. Between the rising of Arcturus and the vernal equinox, they awake in the warmer climates, but even then they still keep within the hives, and have recourse to the provisions kept in reserve for this period. In Italy, however, they do this immediately after the rising of the Vergiliæ, up to which period they are asleep. Some persons, when they take the honey, weigh the hive and all, and remove just as much as they leave: a due sense of equity should always be stringently observed in dealing with them, and it is generally stated that if imposed upon in this division, the swarm will die of grief. It is particularly recommended also that the person who takes the honey should be well washed and clean: bees have a particular aversion, too, to a thief and a menstruous woman. When the honey is taken, it is the best plan to drive away the bees by means of smoke, lest they should become irritated, or else devour the honey themselves. By often applying smoke, too, they are aroused from their idleness to work; but if they have not duly incubated in the comb, it is apt to become of a livid colour. On the other hand, if they are smoked too often, they will become tainted; the honey, too, a substance which turns sour at the very slightest contact with dew, will very quickly receive injury from the taint thus contracted: hence it is that among the various kinds of honey which are preserved, there is one which is known by the name of acapnon.

BEE REPRODUCTION

How bees generate their young has been a subject of great and subtle research among the learned; seeing that no one has ever witnessed any sexual intercourse among these insects. Many persons have expressed an opinion that they must be produced from flowers, aptly and artistically arranged by Nature; while others, again, suppose that they are produced from an intercourse with the one which is to be found in every swarm, and is usually called the king. This one, they say, is the only male in the hive, and is endowed with such extraordinary proportions, that it may not become exhausted in the performance of its duties. Hence it is, that no offspring can be produced without it, all the other bees being females, and attending it in its capacity of a male, and not as their leader. This opinion, however, which is otherwise not improbable, is sufficiently refuted by the generation of the drones. For on what grounds could it possibly happen that the same intercourse should produce an offspring part of which is perfect, and part in an imperfect state? The first surmise which I have mentioned would appear, indeed, to be much nearer the truth, were it not the case that here another difficulty meets us — the circumstance that sometimes, at the extremity of the combs, there are produced bees of a larger size, which put the others to flight. This noxious bee bears the name of œstrus, and how is it possible that it should ever be produced, if it is the fact that the bees themselves form their progeny?

A fact, however, that is well ascertained, is, that bees sit, like the domestic fowl, that which is hatched by them at first having the appearance of a white maggot, and lying across and adhering so tenaciously to the wax as to seem to be part of it. The king, however, from the earliest moment, is of the colour of honey, just as though he were made of the choicest flowers, nor has he at any time the form of a grub, but from the very first is provided with wings. The rest of the bees, as soon as they begin to assume a shape, have the name of nymphæ, while the drones are called sirenes, or cephenes. If a person takes off the head of either kind before the wings are formed, the rest of the body is considered a most choice morsel by the parents. In process of time the parent bees instil nutriment into them, and sit upon them, making on this occasion a loud humming noise, for the purpose, it is generally supposed, of generating that warmth which is so requisite for hatching the young. At length the membrane in which each of them is enveloped, as though it lay in an egg, bursts asunder, and the whole swarm comes to light.

This circumstance was witnessed at the suburban retreat of a man of consular dignity near Rome, whose hives were made of transparent lantern horn: the young were found to be developed in the space of forty-five days. In some combs, there is found what is known by the name of "nail" wax; it is bitter and hard, and is only met with when the bees have failed to hatch their young, either from disease or a natural sterility, it is the abortion, in fact, of the bees. The young ones, the moment they are hatched, commence working with their parents, as though in a course of training, and the newly-born king is accompanied by a multitude of his own age.

That the supply may not run short, each swarm rears several kings; but afterwards, when this progeny begins to arrive at a mature age, with one accord they put to death the inferior ones, lest they should create discord in the swarm. There are two sorts of king bees; those of a reddish colour are better than the black and mottled ones. The kings have always a peculiar form of their own, and are double the size of any of the rest; their wings are shorter than those of the others, their legs are straight, their walk more upright, and they have a white spot on the forehead, which bears some resemblance to a diadem: they differ, too, very much from the rest of the community, in their bright and shining appearance.

MODE OF GOVERNMENT

Let a man employ himself, forsooth, in the enquiry whether there has been only one Hercules, how many fathers Liber there have been, and all the other questions which are buried deep in the mould of antiquity! Here behold a tiny object, one to be met with at most of our country retreats, and numbers of which are always at hand, and yet, after all, it is not agreed among authors whether or not the king is the only one among them that is provided with no sting, and is possessed of no other arms than those afforded him by his majestic office, or whether Nature has granted him a sting, and has only denied him the power of making use of it; it being a well-known fact, that the ruling bee never does use a sting. The obedience which his subjects manifest in his presence is quite surprising. When he goes forth, the whole swarm attends him, throngs about him, surrounds him, protects him, and will not allow him to be seen. At other times, when the swarm is at work within, the king is seen to visit the works, and appears to be giving his encouragement, being himself the only one that is exempt from work: around him are certain other bees which act as body-guards and lictors, the careful guardians of his authority. The king never quits the hive except when the swarm is about to depart; a thing which may be known a long time beforehand, as for some days a peculiar buzzing noise is to be heard within, which denotes that the bees are waiting for a favourable day, and making all due preparations for their departure. On such an occasion, if care is taken to deprive the king of one of his wings, the swarm will not fly away. When they are on the wing, every one is anxious to be near him, and takes a pleasure in being seen in the performance of its duty. When he is weary, they support him on their shoulders; and when he is quite tired, they carry him outright. If one of them falls in the rear from weariness, or happens to go astray, it is able to follow the others by the aid of its acuteness of smell. Wherever the king bee happens to settle, that becomes the encampment of all.

And then, too, it is that they afford presages both of private and public interest, clustering, as they do, like a bunch of grapes, upon houses or temples; presages, in fact, that are often accounted for by great events. Bees settled upon the lips of Plato when still an infant even, announcing thereby the sweetness of that persuasive eloquence for which he was so noted. Bees settled, too, in the camp of the chieftain Drusus when he gained the brilliant victory at Arbalo; a proof, indeed, that the conjectures of soothsayers are not by any means infallible, seeing that they are of opinion that this is always of evil augury. When their leader is withheld from them, the swarm can always be detained; and when lost, it will disperse and take its departure to find other kings. Without a king, in fact, they cannot exist, and it is with the greatest reluctance that they put them to death when there are several; they prefer, too, to destroy the cells of the young ones, if they find reason to despair of providing food; in such case they then expel the drones. And yet, with regard to the last, I find that some doubts are entertained; and that there are some authors who are of opinion that they form a peculiar species, like that bee, the very largest among them all, which is known by the name of the "thief," because it furtively devours the honey; it is distinguished by its black colour and the largeness of its body. It is a well-known fact, however, that the bees are in the habit of killing the drones. These last have no king of their own; but how it is that they are produced without a sting, is a matter still undetermined.

In a wet spring the young swarms are more numerous; in a dry one the honey is most abundant. If food happens to fail the inhabitants of any particular hive, the swarm makes a concerted attack upon a neighbouring one, with the view of plundering it. The swarm that is thus attacked, at once ranges itself in battle array, and if the bee-keeper should happen to be present, that side which perceives itself favoured by him will refrain from attacking him. They often fight, too, for other reasons as well, and the two generals are to be seen drawing up their ranks in battle array against their opponents. The dispute generally arises in culling from the flowers, when each, the moment that it is in danger, summons its companions to its aid. The battle, however, is immediately put an end to by throwing dust among them, or raising a smoke; and if milk or honey mixed with water is placed before them, they speedily become reconciled.

KINDS OF BEES

There are field bees also, and wild bees, ungainly in appearance, and much more irascible than the others, but remarkable for their laboriousness and the excellence of their work. Of domestic bees there are two sorts; the best are those with short bodies, speckled all over, and of a compact round shape. Those that are long, and resemble the wasp in appearance, are an inferior kind; and of these last, the very worst of all are those which have the body covered with hair. In Pontus there is a kind of white bee, which makes honey twice a month. On the banks of the river Thermodon there are two kinds found, one of which makes honey in the trees, the other under ground: they form a triple row of combs, and produce honey in the greatest abundance.

Nature has provided bees with a sting, which is inserted in the abdomen of the insect. There are some who think that at the first blow which they inflict with this weapon they will instantly die, while others, again, are of opinion that such is not the case, unless the animal drives it so deep as to cause a portion of the intestines to follow; and they assert, also, that after they have thus lost their sting they become drones, and make no honey, being thus castrated, so to say, and equally incapable of inflicting injury, and of making themselves useful by their labours. We have instances stated of horses being killed by bees.

They have a great aversion to bad smells, and fly away from them; a dislike which extends to artificial perfumes even. Hence it is that they will attack persons who smell of unguents. They themselves, also, are exposed to the attacks of wasps and hornets, which belong to the same class, but are of a degenerate nature; these wage continual warfare against them, as also does a species of gnat, which is known by the name of "mulio;" swallows, too, and various other birds prey upon them. Frogs lie in wait for them when in quest of water, which, in fact, is their principal occupation at the time they are rearing their young. And it is not only the frog that frequents ponds and streams that is thus injurious to them, but the bramble-frog as well, which will come to the hives even in search of them, and, crawling up to the entrance, breathe through the apertures; upon hearing which, a bee flies to the spot, and is snapped up in an instant. It is generally stated that frogs are proof against the sting of the bee. Sheep, too, are peculiarly dangerous to them, as they have the greatest difficulty in extricating themselves from the fleece. The smell of crabs, if they happen to be cooked in their vicinity, is fatal to them.

DISEASES

Bees are also by nature liable to certain diseases of their own. The sign that they are diseased, is a kind of torpid, moping sadness: on such occasions, they are to be seen bringing out those that are sick before the hives, and placing them in the warm sun, while others, again, are providing them with food. Those that are dead they carry away from the hive, and attend the bodies, paying their last duties, as it were, in funeral procession. If the king should happen to be carried off by the pestilence, the swarm remains plunged in grief and listless inactivity; it collects no more food, and ceases to issue forth from its abode; the only thing that it does is to gather around the body, and to emit a melancholy humming noise. Upon such occasions, the usual plan is to disperse the swarm and take away the body; for otherwise they would continue listlessly gazing upon it, and so prolong their grief. Indeed, if due care is not taken to come to their aid, they will die of hunger. It is from their cheerfulness, in fact, and their bright and sleek appearance that we usually form an estimate as to their health.

There are certain maladies, also, which affect their productions; when they do not fill their combs, the disease under which they are labouring is known by the name of claros, and if they fail to rear their young, they are suffering from the effects of that known as blapsigonia.

HARMFUL THINGS

Echo, or the noise made by the reverberation of the air, is also injurious to bees, as it dismays them by its redoubled sounds; fogs, also, are noxious to them. Spiders, too, are especially hostile to bees; when they have gone so far as to build their webs within the hive, the death of the whole swarm is the result. The common and ignoble moth, too, that is to be seen fluttering about a burning candle, is deadly to them, and that in more ways than one. It devours the wax, and leaves its ordure behind it, from which the maggot known to us as the "teredo" is produced; besides which, wherever it goes, it drops the down from off its wings, and thereby thickens the threads of the cobwebs. The teredo is also engendered in the wood of the hive, and then it proves especially destructive to the wax. Bees are the victims, also, of their own greediness, for when they glut themselves overmuch with the juices of the flowers, in the spring season more particularly, they are troubled with flux and looseness. Olive oil is fatal to not only bees, but all other insects as well, and more especially if they are placed in the sun, after the head has been immersed in it. Sometimes, too, they themselves are the cause of their own destruction; as, for instance, when they see preparations being made for taking their honey, and immediately fall to devouring it with the greatest avidity. In other respects they are remarkable for their abstemiousness, and they will expel those that are inclined to be prodigal and voracious, no less than those that are sluggish and idle. Their own honey even may be productive of injury to them; for if they are smeared with it on the fore-part of the body, it is fatal to them. Such are the enemies, so numerous are the accidents — and how small a portion of them have I here enumerated! — to which a creature that proves so bountiful to us is exposed. In the appropriate place we will treat of the proper remedies; for the present the nature of them is our subject.

KEEPING BEES TO THE HIVE

The clapping of the hands and the tinkling of brass afford bees great delight, and it is by these means that they are brought together; a strong proof, in fact, that they are possessed of the sense of hearing. When their work is completed, their offspring brought forth, and all their duties fulfilled, they still have certain formal exercises to perform, ranging abroad throughout the country, and soaring aloft in the air, wheeling round and round as they fly, and then, when the hour for taking their food has come, returning home. The extreme period of their life, supposing that they escape accident and the attacks of their enemies, is only seven years; a hive, it is said, never lasts more than ten. There are some persons, who think that, when dead, if they are preserved in the house throughout the winter, and then exposed to the warmth of the spring sun, and kept hot all day in the ashes of fig-tree wood, they will come to life again.

RENEWING THE SWARM

These persons say also, that if the swarm is entirely lost, it may be replaced by the aid of the belly of an ox newly killed, covered over with dung. Virgil also says that this may be done with the body of a young bull, in the same way that the carcase of the horse produces wasps and hornets, and that of the ass beetles, Nature herself effecting these changes of one substance into another. But in all these last, sexual intercourse is to be perceived as well, though the characteristics of the offspring are pretty much the same as those of the bee.

CHAPTER II

BEES IN COLUMELLA'S

DE RE RUSTICA

I Come now to the management of bee-hives, concerning which no precepts can be given with greater diligence, than have been already delivered by Hyginus ; nor more gracefully and handsomely, than by Virgil ; nor more elegantly, than by Celsus. Hyginus has industriously collected the sentiments of ancient authors, that were dispersed in their writings, which were unknown to the world. Virgil has illuminated them with flowers of poetry ; Celsus has adapted and made use of the manner of both these mentioned authors : wherefore we would not have so much as attempted to discourse of this subject, but that the consummation of the profession we have undertaken required the handling of this part of it also, lest the body of the work, which we have begun, should appear maimed and imperfect, as if some member were cut off from it. And I would rather allow to poetical licence, than to our belief, those things which have been fabulously related concerning the origination of bees, which Hyginus has not past over. Nor, indeed, is it worthy of an Husbandman, to inquire whether there ever was such a woman as Melissa , of a most exquisite beauty, which Jupiter transformed into a bee ; or whether (as Euhemerus the Poet says) bees were bred of hornets and the fun, which the Phryxonian nymphs educated ; and that soon afterwards they became nurses to Jupiter in the Dictæan cave ; and, by the free gift of the god, they obtained the same food for their own sustenance, wherewith they had brought up their little softer-child : for, tho' these things are not unbecoming a poet, nevertheless Virgil touched upon them slightly, and very briefly, only in one small verse: In Dicte's cave they fed the king of heaven.

But neither does that indeed belong to Husbandmen ; when, and in what country, they were first: produced, whether in Thessaly under Aristæus ; or in the island of Cea, as Euhemerus writes ; or in the times of Erichthonius, in mount Hymettus, as Euthronius ; or in the times of Saturn of Crete, as Nicander says, no more, than whether the swarms procreate their offspring by coupling together, as we see other animals do ; or choose the heir of their family from among the flowers, which our Maro affirms ; and whether they vomit the liquid honey out of their mouth, or yield it from any other part of their body; for it rather belongs to the searchers into the secret and hidden things of nature, than to Husbandmen, to inquire after these and such-like things. Also these things are more agreeable to men of study and learning, who have leisure to read, than to Husbandmen, who are full of business; because they neither assist them in their work, nor contribute any thing to increase their estate.

KINDS OF BEES
& WHICH OF THEM IS THE BEST

Wherefore let us return to those things which are more proper for them who have bee-hives under their care and management. Aristotle, the founder of the Peripatetic sect, in those books which he wrote of animals, shows, that there are several kinds of bees, or of swarms of bees; and that some of those swarms have bees that are exceeding large, but round and compact, and the same black and shaggy;

others lesser indeed, but equally round, and of a dusky colour, with horrid grisly hair ; and others of a smaller size, but not so round, but nevertheless fat, and broad, and of a somewhat better colour: and they have some that are very small and slender, with the trunk of their belly sharp, and drawing to a point, of diverse colours, somewhat shining like gold, light and nimble. And Virgil, following his authority, approves most of such as are very small, oblong, smooth and nimble, bright and shining:

> "Whose bodies, marked with pairs of spots like drops
> "Of liquid gold, a dazzling light:"

Of gentle and mild dispositions; for by how much the greater, and rounder also, the bee is, by so much the worse it is: but if it be of a more fierce and cruel temper, it is by much the worst of all. But, nevertheless, the angry disposition of bees of a better character is easily mitigated and softened by the continual intervention of those who take care of the bee-hives; for they grow quickly tame when they are often handled, and endure for ten years, if they are carefully managed : nor can any swarm of bees exceed this age, although they yearly substitute young ones in the room of those that are dead; for, in the tenth year, almost the whole family, that lives together in one hive, is consumed, and reduced to utter destruction. Therefore, lest that should be the case of the whole apiary, a new race must be constantly propagated ; and, in the spring, you must carefully observe when the new swarms issue forth in great numbers, that they may be received, and the number of their dwelling-houses increased : for they are often seized with diseases. After what manner the same must be cured, shall be declared in its proper place.

In the mean while, having made choice of bees according to the marks we have now mentioned, you ought to designate proper places for them to gather their food; and let them be the most retired that can be had ; and, as our Maro directs, void of cattle, and in such a situation as is exposed to the Sun, and sheltered from stormy weather ;

> 'Where winds have no access; for winds impede
> 'Their course, when with their food they're homeward-
> bound,
> 'Where neither Sheep, nor frisking kids, insult
> 'The flowers; nor heifers, rambling over the fields,
> 'Shake off the dew, and crush the rising herb.'

Let the same quarter also be abundantly productive of small shrubs, and especially of thyme, or bastard marjoram, as also of thymbra, or Greek savory, or our own Italian savory, which the country-people call satureia : after these, let there be abundance of shrubs of a greater growth, as rosemary, and the cytisus or shrub-trefoil, of both sorts: for there is one sort of it that is sown or planted, and another sort which grows of its own accord. And, likewise, the ever-green pine, and the lesser ever-green oak ; for the taller one is dis-approved by all: ivy-trees also are received, not for their goodness, but because they yield very much honey. But, the most approved trees are, the bright-red and white jujube-tree, likewise the amaranth, as also walnut-trees, peach-trees, and pear-trees; in a word, the greatest part of pomiferous trees, that I may not insist upon each of them. But, of forest or wild trees, the most suitable and convenient for them are the mad-bearing red oaks, as also the turpentine-tree, and the mastic-tree, which is not unlike to this, and the sweet-smelling cedar : but of all, the lime- or linden-trees alone are hurtful to them; yew-trees are entirely rejected. Moreover, a thousand plants, which either spring up and flourish upon the uncultivated turf, or are cultivated and improved with the furrow, produce flowers exceeding friendly to bees; as are the shrubs of the Italian starwort in well-watered ground, acanthus stalks, the stem of the asphodel or king's-spear, the sword-like leaves of the daffodil. But the white lilies, planted in the garden-ridge, make a bright appearance ; nor are the white violets or stock gilliflowers inferior to these in beauty; also scarlet roses, and yellowish and purple violets ; and likewise the sky-coloured hyacinth; also the Corycian and Sicilian saffron-bulb is planted, in order to give colour and flavour to the honey.

Moreover, innumerable herbs of a baser character spring up, both in cultivated and in pasture-lands, which furnish and replenish the honey-combs with abundance of wax ; as the lapsanœ , or common wild cabbage; and, which is not more precious than these, the horseradish, and the charlock, or potherbs like the wild mustard, the flowers of wild endive, and black poppy ; also the wild parsnip, and the cultivated one of the same name, which the Greeks call σταφυλῖνον. But of all these I have mentioned, and of those which I have omitted, endeavouring to save time, (for their number could not be reckoned up) thyme gives the most exquisite taste to honey: then the next is thymbra, Greek savory, and oregano. At third place, but yet exceeding good, is rosemary, and our own Italian savory, which I call satureia. The honey will be of mediocre taste if collected from   tamarisk and jujube flowers. But, of all, honey from the woods, which comes of the broom-tree, and the strawberry-tree, and farmstead honey also, collected from plants that grow in the garden and in dunghills, are reckoned of the very worst character. And since I have described the situation of their pastures, and also their several sorts of food, I shall now speak of the receptacles of the swarms, and of their little dwelling-houses.

31

The hive must be placed to the Sun during winter, far from tumult, and crowds of men and cattle, in a place neither warm nor cold; for both the one, and the other, is very troublesome to them. But let it be in the lower part of a valley, that both the empty bees, when they go forth to forage, or to gather their food, may fly up the more easily to the higher grounds; and, having gathered such things as are proper for their use, may fly down through the steep places, with their burden, without any difficulty. If the situation of the farmstead offers these conditions, do not doubt, but join the hive to the building, and surround it with a wall; but it must be in that part which is free from the noisome smells of the toilets, the dunghill, and the baths.

If it is not possible to find a better location, it will be necessary—as long as there are no greater disadvantages—that the hive be thus placed, and be under the eyes of the owner.

But, if all things be unfriendly, pitch upon a neighbouring valley, to which the possessor may frequently go down without any great trouble : for that business requires the greatest fidelity; which, because it is exceeding rare, is better secured and preserved by the owner's coming unawares. Nor does it only hate and abhor a fraudulent Overseer and Manager, but slothfulness also, which produces nastiness: for it is equally provoked and offended with dirty and slovenly treatment, as with fraudulent management.

But, where-ever the bee-hives shall be placed, let them not be inclosed with a very high wall ; and if, through fear of robbers, you are better pleased with one that is higher, let it be passable for the bees, with small windows, all in a row, three feet high from the ground ; and let a cottage be joined to it, wherein both the Keepers may dwell, and the implements be laid up : and let it be chiefly replenished with hives prepared before-hand for the use of the young swarms, as also with wholesome medicinal herbs ; and if there be any other things which are applied to such as are sick and languishing.

> ' And let the palm, or huge wild-olive tree
> ' Overshade the porch, that, when new kings lead south
> ' The first-hatched swarms; and when the sportive youth,
> ' From close confinement freed, shall, in the spring,
> ' Make sallies from their hives, and play all round ;
> ' The neighbouring bank may, from the scorching heat,
> ' Invite them to retire; and the obvious tree
> ' With verdant leafy shelters stop their flight.'

Then let continually running water, if you have the conveniency of it, be conveyed into it; or let it be given by hand in a canal or trough, built for that purpose, without which neither the honey-combs, nor the honey, nor the young bees, can be formed. Whether therefore, as I said, water that is constantly running by, or well-water, be sent into them by canals, let there be piles of stones and rods raised in it for the conveniency of the bees ;

> ' That on these frequent bridges they may stand
> ' Secure, and to the summer-fun expand
> ' Their wings, if chance the east wind's headlong blast
> ' Has sprinkled, or has plunged them in the deep.'

Then around the whole apiary ought to be planted little trees of small growth, especially for their wholesomeness: such as the cytisus, the cassia, pine-trees, and rosemary, as they are a remedy for them when they are languishing ; as also bushes of satury and thyme; as also those of violets, or whatever other things the quality of the ground suffers to be usefully planted. Let not only green things of a disagreeable and noisome smell, but also all other things whatsoever, of the same quality, be kept at a distance from them; such as

33

the smell of a crab, when it is burnt in the fire ; or the smell of mud and dirt taken out of a marsh. Likewise let hollow rocks, or shrill loud-sounding valleys, which the Greeks call ἠχοῦς (echoes) be avoided.

APPROVED BEEHIVES

Therefore, when their place has been established, bee-hives must be fabricated according to the condition and circumstances of the country. For if it be fertile of the cork-tree, without any doubt we may make very useful hives of its bark, because they are neither extremely cold in winter, nor exceeding hot in summer : or, if it abounds in giant fennels, of these also vases are woven with equal conveniency, as they are like to the nature of bark. If neither of these is ready at hand, they join willows together, and weave them like weavers work: and, if these cannot be had, they must be made of the wood of a tree made hollow, or sawn into boards. Those made of potters earth have the very worst quality of any ; for the summer-heats set them on fire, and they are frozen with the winter-colds.

There are two other kinds of hives remaining, which may either be made of dung, or built of brick : one of which Celsus very justly disapproved, because it is very obnoxious to fire; the other he approved, though he did not dissemble its chiefest disadvantage, viz. that, if there should be occasion for it, it cannot be removed from one place to another: therefore I do not agree with him who thinks, that, notwithstanding this inconveniency, bee-hives of this kind ought to be had for not only is it repugnant to the interest of the owner, that they be such as cannot be removed, when at any time he may have a mind either to sell them, or to furnish other grounds with them (for this conveniency relates only to the advantage of the Master of the family); but as to what ought to be done for the advantage, and on the account, of the bees themselves, when they are afflicted either with a distemper, or with the barrenness and penury of the place; and it may be proper, that they be sent into another quarter; and they cannot be moved for the foresaid reason ; this is principally to be avoided. Therefore, although I reverence the authority of that most learned man, yet, setting aside all ambition, I have not omitted to declare my own opinion : for that which chiefly moves Celsus , viz. lest the bee-stalls be liable either to fire or thieves, may be avoided by building a brick-work round the hives, that an obstacle may be put to the rapaciousness of the robber, and the hives be protected against the violence of fire : and when it is necessary to move them, and carry them to another place, it may be done by loosening the joinings of the structure.

PLACING BEEHIVES

But because most people think, that this requires too much labour and pains, therefore whatever sort of hives they shall think most proper to be placed, there ought to be a bank of stone extended through the whole apiary, three feet in height, and as many in thickness ; and, when it is thus built, it ought to be carefully smoothed with plaster, that there may be no way for lizards, or serpents, or other noxious animals, to climb up to them. Then upon this bank are placed, either as Celsus directs hives made of bricks, or, as we are best pleased with, hives with brick-work built around them, except behind: or, which is the common practice with all people, who are diligent and careful about these things, there are vases placed all in a row, which are fastened and bound either with small bricks, or with rough stone and mortar, so that each of them is contained within two narrow walls, and the back- and fore-parts are open and free: for sometimes they must be laid open both on that side where the bees go forth, and much more on the back-side, because the swarms are cured from time to time.

But if no walls are built between the hives, nevertheless they must be so placed, that they may be a little distant from each other, lest, when they are viewed and looked into, that which is handled in the cleaning and curing of it, should shake the other, which sticks close to it, and bruise the neighbouring bees, which are afraid of every motion given to their weak wax-works, as of ruin and destruction to them. It is sufficient indeed, that there be three rows of vases built up in height one above the other, because even so the person that cures them cannot very conveniently look into the uppermost.

Let the mouths of the hives, which afford entries to the bees, lean more downward, and be more sloping, than their backs, that the rains may not flow into them ; and if, notwithstanding, they chance to get in, that they may not remain there, but run out by the entry: for which reason it is proper, that the hives be fenced and secured with porches above the entries: if otherwise, they must be shadowed with green boughs daubed over with Carthaginian clay, which covering keeps out both the colds, and the rains and the heats. Nevertheless the burning heat is not so hurtful to this kind of animals as the winter is: therefore let there always be a building behind the apiary, which may receive the injury of the north wind, and give a moderate heat to the bee-hives. Likewise the hives themselves, although they be protected by the building, ought to be so placed, as to be directly opposite to the sun-rising in winter, that so the bees may have the benefit of the warmth of the fun when they go out in the morning, and may be thereby the more brisk and active ; for cold begets sluggishness: for which reason also the holes, by which they go out and come in, ought to be very strait, that they may admit as little cold as possible: and it is sufficient, that they be so bored, that they may not receive more than one bee at its full growth. So neither the poisonous newt, nor the unlucky and mischievous kind of beetle or butterfly, nor the light-shunning wood-louse, as Maro says, plunder the honey-combs through the gate, when it is wider and larger than it ought to be. And it is a very great advantage, that, in proportion to the number of bees in the bee-hive, there be two or three passages made in the same cover, at some distance the one from the other, to guard against the deceit and craft of the lizard, who, like a watch or keeper of the entry, and gaping for his prey, with open mouth destroys the bees as they go out; and fewer of them perish when they are at liberty to avoid the snares of this pest, that besieges them, by escaping through another passage.

PURCHASING BEES & CAPTURING WILD SWARMS

What we have said may suffice concerning the choosing of pastures, dwelling-houses, and seats for them; which being provided, the next thing we are to do is to seek for swarms: and they come to us either by purchase, or by free gift. But such of them as we shall purchase with money, let us try, and approve them more carefully by the foresaid marks: and let us consider how numerous they are before we buy them, by opening the hives, and looking into them: or, if we cannot conveniently look into them, doubtless we shall mark what we can cast our eyes upon, whether there are very many of them standing in the porch of the gate, and a vehement sound be heard of those that are humming within doors; and also (if peradventure they are all silent, and at rest within their dwelling-house) we may make an estimate either of the greatness or smallness of their number, from the sudden noise and murmuring, that will follow upon our having applied our lips to the holes of the entry, and breathed strongly into them.

But we must especially be careful, that they be brought rather from the neighbourhood than from distant regions, because they use to be highly provoked with the strangeness of the climate. But if this cannot be obtained, and we be under the necessity of carrying them long journeys, we must take care, that they be not disturbed and made uneasy by the ruggedness of the roads: and it will be best to carry them upon one's shoulders in the night-time ; for in the day-time they must have rest given them ; and such liquors as are acceptable to the bees must be poured into the hives, whereby they may be nourished within their enclosures. Then after they are brought home, if the day come upon you sooner than you expected, the hive must neither be opened, nor placed in the bee-stall, except in the evening, that the bees may go out peaceable and quiet in the morning, after they have rested the whole night: and we ought to be upon the watch for the space of three days almost, to observe if they sally out all in a body ; which when they do, they are contriving to make their escape : we must presently give orders for such remedies as ought to be made use of, in order to put a stop to them. But such as come into our hands, either in presents, or which we catch by surprise, are not so scrupulously inquired into: although even in that manner, I would not have any in my possession but the very best ; seeing both the good and the bad require the same expense, and the same labour of a Keeper: and, which is of very great importance, the base and degenerate, which may bring infamy and reproach upon those that are of a generous kind, must not be intermixed with them ; for the produce of honey is less than you expected, when more slothful and idle swarms intervene.

Nevertheless, because sometimes, by reason of the nature and circumstances of the places, we must provide ourselves even with cattle that are but indifferent, (for, to be sure, that which is bad is by no means to be provided) we must use our endeavours to search out the swarms after this manner: Where-ever there are forests proper for making of honey, there is nothing that the bees do sooner, than to make choice of the neighbouring fountains, which they may make use of. Therefore it is proper to cover them, for the most part, from the second hour of the day, and to watch what numbers of them come to fetch water: for, if there are few of them that fly about, (except there be several heads of rivulets, which make them thinner, when they are separated from one another) they give us to understand, that there is a scarcity of them; by reason of which we will suspect, that the place is not productive of honey. But, if they assemble in great numbers, they give us also greater hopes of catching swarms of them, and they are found out after this manner:

First, we must search, and find out, how far off they are; and for this purpose a liquid red ochre must be prepared, wherewith having tinged some straws, or stalks of herbs, when with the same you touch the backs of the bees that sip in the fountains, if you stay in the same place, you will the more easily know them, when they come back; and if they make no great stay, you may know, that they have their abode in the neighbourhood : but, if they be a long while before they return, you shall make an estimate of the distance of the place according to the time of their delay. But, if you observe, that they return quick, if, with no great difficulty, you can follow them in the way they fly, you shall be easily conduced to the place where the swarm has its place.

But you must make use of more skill and prudence, with respect to those which shall be seen to go farther off; which is such as this: You must cut off an entire joint of a reed with its own knots, and bore a hole in the side of the cutting; and, having dropped a little honey, or soaked must, into it through the said hole, you must place it hard by the fountain: then, when, at the smell of the sweet liquor, several bees shall have crept into it, you must take up the cutting;

and, having put your thumb upon the hole, you must let out only one of them at a time, which, after it has made its escape, shows the Observer the place to which it directs its course; and he, as long as he can hold it out, pursues it as it flies away : then, when he loses sight of the bee, he sends out another; and if it flies towards the same part of the heaven, he continues to pursue in the same path ; but if otherwise, he suffers one after another to go out at the open hole : and let him mark the quarter towards which most of them fly, and pursue them, till he be brought to the lurking-hole of the whole swarm.

But, if the swarm be hid in a cave, you may fetch them out with smoke; and, when they have sallied out, you check and stop them with the noise of brass: for, being presently terrified with the sound, they will fit down either upon a shrub, or on an higher bough of a tree ; and the person that searches for them, and finds them out, puts them up in a vase prepared for that purpose. But if they have taken up their place in an hollow tree, and if either the branch, which they have seated themselves upon, stands out from the body of the tree, or they are in the very trunk of the tree itself, then, if the moderate size of it will allow it, first the upper-part of it, which is empty of bees, is cut off with a very sharp saw, that it may be done the sooner; then the lower part also, as far as it seems to be inhabited. Then, after it is cut through at both ends, it is covered over with a clean garment; for this also is of very great importance ; and, if it has any gaping chinks, you fill them up with clay, and so bring it to the place : and, some small holes in it (as I said already) being left open, it is placed in the same manner as the rest of the bee-hives.

But it is proper, that the person, who makes it his business to search for them, and find them out, make choice of the morning-tide, that he may have the whole day before him to spy out the places where the bees frequent, and go and come. For often, if he has begun to observe them too late, when they have their place in the neighbourhood, they retire, after they have finished their ordinary task of work, and do not return to the water ; whereby it comes to pass, that the person who searches for them is ignorant how far the swarm is distant from the fountain. There are some who, in the beginning of the spring, gather mint, and (as the foresaid poet says)

'Bruised balm, and honeywort's ignoble grafs;'

And other-like herbs, wherewith this kind of animals is delighted and so rub the hives throughly with them, that the smell and the juice of them may stick to the vessel; which, when they have cleaned them, they sprinkle again with a little honey, and place them up and down the woods not far from the fountains; and, when they are filled with swarms, they carry them home. But it is not expedient to do this, except in places where there is abundance of bees; for often they who by chance pass by, when they find the empty vessels, carry them away with them: nor is the obtaining one or two full ones of so great account, as to compensate the loss of several empty ones. But in a greater plenty, although many of them are intercepted, yet more is acquired by the bees that are found: and this is the method of catching wild swarms of bees.

OBSERVING AND PLACING INTO HIVES

Moreover, there is such another method of retaining the swarms that are bred in our own country. The Keeper, indeed, ought always carefully to go round the bee-hives; for there is no time wherein they do not want his care and management: but they require a more punctual and diligent attendance, when they swarm in the spring, and their new offspring breaks out of their hives, which cannot contain them; and unless the Overseer constantly besieges them, and presently receives and entertains them, the young ones make their escape; because, such is the nature of bees, that every commonalty is generated at the same time with their kings, which, as soon as they have got strength to fly out of their hives, disdain and despise the company, and the society, of their seniors, and much more their government and command : for as mankind, endued with reason, will not allow of any partnership in the regal power, far less will these dumb animals, who are destitute of counsel.

Therefore the new chieftains come forth with their youth, which remaining conglomerated for one or two days in the very porch of their dwelling-house, by their coming out of it they show, that they desire to have a place of their own ; and if one be presently assigned them by their Keeper, they are satisfied with it, as if it were their native country. But if the Keeper be out of the way, and neglects it, they go to a strange country, as if they were wrongfully cast out of their own. To prevent this, it is the business of a good Overseer to have his eyes upon the hives, during the spring-time, almost till the eighth hour of the day, after which the young swarms do not precipitantly withdraw themselves; and carefully to watch and observe both when they go out, and when they return; for there are some, which, breaking out all of a sudden, steal away without any delay.

He may certainly find out, and know beforehand, their intended flight, by applying his ear to each of the hives in the evening: for so it is, that almost for three days before they design to make an eruption, there arises a tumult, and confused noise and murmur among them, as of an army going to march: from which, as Virgil says very truly,

> ' Tis easy to foreknow the vulgar's minds:
> ' For such as loitering stand, the martial found
> ' Of the hoarse brass reproves; likewise a voice

    ' Is heard, which imitates the broken sounds
    ' Of trumpets.'

Therefore the hives that do this ought especially to be observed, that whether they shall sally out to battle, (for they
often fight amongst themselves, as in civil wars, and with
other hives, as with foreign nations) or break out all of a
sudden, in order to make their escape, the Keeper may be
present, ready prepared for both events.

A quarrel, indeed, either of one hive disagreeing among
themselves, or of two hives at variance the one with the other, is easily quelled: for, as the same poet says,

    ' With throwing of small dust the strife is checked,
    ' And ceases'—

Or with raisin-wine, or honeyed-wine, or any other such-
like liquor sprinkled upon them : for so it is, that the sweetness of these things, being familiar to them, appeases their
wrath, when they are in a rage. For the same things also
have a wonderful influence to reconcile the kings that are at
variance : for often there are more captains of one people,
and by the sedition, as it were, of the nobility, the common
people is divided into factions, which must not be suffered
to happen frequently, because whole nations are consumed
by intestine wars. Therefore, if the princes be in friendship
and favour with one another, peace continues without
bloodshed: but, if you shall observe them very often engaged
in a pitched battle, you shall take care to kill the ring-leaders
of the seditions ; but by the foresaid remedies, their battles
and quarrels are composed. And, furthermore, when a great
multitude of them fits down all in a lump, upon the next
branch of a green leafy little tree, observe whether the whole
swarm hangs down from it like one duller of grapes: and
this shall be a sign, either that there is only one king among

them ; or that, if there be more of them, they are heartily reconciled ; which you may suffer to continue so, till they fly back again to their own habitation.

But if the swarm be divided and distinguished, resembling two, or several udders, you need not doubt that there are several rulers among them, and that they are angry: and you ought to search for their captains in those parts wherein you see the bees are assembled and conglomerated in greatest numbers. Therefore, having anointed your hand with the juice of the fore-mentioned herbs, that is, of lemon balm or lemongrass, lest they run away when you touch them, you must put in your fingers gently among them ; and, having separated the bees from one another, you must search till you find the author of the quarrel, whom you ought to squeeze to death.

THE FORM OF THE KING OF BEES

But these kings are a little larger and more oblong than the other bees, with straighter legs, but not so large wings, of a beautiful bright-shining colour, brisk and nimble, and without hair, without a sting, unless any think, that the fuller hair, as it were, which they carry in their belly, is their sting; and even of this itself they make no use to hurt. Some of them also are found of a dusky colour, and bristly, whose disposition and temper you may condemn from the habit and make of their body.

> ' Two sorts of features, and two different forms
> ' Of bodies, have the kings, which rule this folk :
> ' The one with spots of glistering gold adorned,
> ' And with bright-shining scales, and comely face,
> ' In splendid state appears.'

And this, which is the best of the two, is most approved; for the worst, like sordid spittle, is as ugly and ill-favoured as

' The traveller, who comes from depths of dust,
' And from his parched mouth spits moistened earth : '

And, as the same poet says,

' With sloth inglorious drags his spacious paunch.'

Therefore all the Generals of a baser character

' Destroy, and let the better Prince bear sway,
' And reign without a rival in his court.'

Nevertheless he himself must be stripped of his wings, when he often makes eruptions with his swarm, and endeavours to run away: for, having pulled off his wings, we shall retain the vagabond General, as it were, with a chain at his foot; who, being deprived of all means of making his escape, will not dare to go without the bounds of his kingdom ; for which reason he does not indeed allow the people of his dominion to ramble up and down, and wander at a greater distance from him.

INCREASING THE BEEHIVE POPULATION

But sometimes the King must be put to death, when the old bee-hive has not a sufficient number of bees; and its want of number must be supplied by some other swarm. Therefore, when, in the beginning of the spring, a numerous young brood has been hatched in that hive, the new King must be squeezed to death, that the multitude may continue to live with their parents without discord. But if the honey-combs shall have produced no progeny at all, you may bring the commonalty of two or three hives together into one ; but they must be first sprinkled with sweet liquor: then afterwards you may shut them up, and, having placed meat for them, you may keep them shut up almost for the space of three days, leaving small breathing-places for them, till they accustom themselves to converse familiarly, and live together.

There are some who may rather chose to put the older King out of the way, which proves very hurtful ; because the more aged multitude, if he be put to death, must of necessity, like a number of old senators, obey those that are younger than themselves ; and, if there be any of them that obstinately despise the commands of those that are stronger, they are punished, and put to death.

Nevertheless this inconveniency usually befalls a younger swarm, when the King of the ancienter bees, which was left by us, fails, and, through old age, becomes unable to govern, that the family falls into discord from too great licentiousness, as if their Lord were dead. To which a remedy is easily applied : for out of those hives, which have several kings, one General is chosen ; and, being translated to those bees which are without any government, is constituted their ruler. But the paucity of the bees may be remedied with less trouble, in those dwellings which labour under any pestilential distemper: for after the havoc and definition of the hive, reduced to a small number, is known, you must examine and view what honey-combs it has: then, afterwards, from the wax which contains the feeds of the young bees, you must cut away that part wherein the offspring of the royal kind is animated : for this is easy to be seen because, at the very end of the wax-works, there appears, as it were, the nipple of a pap rising higher, and of a wider cavity than the rest of the holes are of wherein the young bees of vulgar note are contained. Celsus indeed affirms, that, in the outmost honey-combs, there are transverse pipes or cavities, which contain the young royal progeny. Hyginus also, following the authority of the Greeks , denies that the Captain-general is formed of a little worm or maggot (as the rest of the bees are); but that in the circumference of the honey-combs there are found straight holes, somewhat larger than those of the Plebeian feed, filled, as it were, with a sordid substance of a red colour, out of which the winged King is at first immediately formed.

PUTTING BEES IN THE HIVE
& HINDERING THEIR ESCAPE

There is also that care which is to be taken of a swarm bred in our own bee-stall, if by chance they should grow weary of, and abhor, their native country ; and, by making an eruption at the foresaid time, declare their intention of betaking themselves by flight to a more distant habitation. And the hive gives intimation of this, when the bee so avoids the porch of her house, that not one of them flies back to it, but presently raises herself to a greater height. Let the youth that are making their escape be terrified with brazen timbrels, or rattles, or with the found of earthen vessels, or tiles, which, for the most part, lie every-where : and when, after they are frightened, they either return to their maternal hive, and hang all in a clew in the entry to it, or presently betake themselves to the next green leafy bough; let the Keeper presently rub and anoint all over a new hive, prepared for that purpose, with the foresaid herbs: then having sprinkled it with drops of honey, let him apply it to them ; then, gathering the bees together, let him put them into it, either with his hands, or with a bowl: and after all other due care has been taken, and the vase has been carefully adjusted and daubed over, let him suffer it, in the mean while, to remain in the same place, till it draws towards evening ; then, in the beginning of the twilight, let him remove it thence, and place it in the row of the other hives.

But it is necessary also to have empty houses placed for them in the apiary : for there are some hives which, as soon as they come forth, presently seek for a seat for themselves in the neighbourhood, and take possession of that which they find empty. This is almost a complete account of the care that is necessary both for acquiring and retaining of bees.

BEE DISEASES REMEDIES

The next thing is to inquire after remedies for sick bees, or are afflicted with the plague. The plague rarely proves destructive to bees: nevertheless I do not find that any other thing can be done, than that which we directed with respect to other sorts of cattle, that the hives be removed to some distant place. But, in these, both the causes of their diseases are more easily discerned, and their remedies found out. But their greatest annual distemper is in the beginning of the spring, when the young sprigs of spurge blossom, and the elms disclose their feeds; for as with new apples, so they are alluded with these primitive flowers; and they feed greedily upon them after their winter hunger, such food being no otherwise hurtful to them but their eating of it to excess, with which having glutted themselves, they die of a looseness, unless they have speedy relief; for spurge gives a looseness to other animals also, but elms particularly to bees: and this is the reason why bees seldom continue numerous in the regions of Italy, which are planted with trees of this kind. Therefore in the beginning of the spring, if you give them medicated food, by the same remedies you may both prevent their being afflicted with such a plague, and they may be cured when they are seized with it.

For as to what Hyginus , who followed authors that lived before his time, has delivered, I myself dare not affirm it, not having made the experiment; nevertheless they who have a mind to it may try it. For he directs us about the time of the vernal equinox, when the clemency of the day invites, after the third hour, to bring forth, and expose to the Sun, the bodies of those bees, which, when such a plague has seized them, are found killed in heaps under the honeycombs, and have been laid up in a dry place during the winter, and to cover them over with fig-tree ashes; which being done, he affirms, that, within two hours, being animated with the enlivening steam of the heat, and having resumed their spirit, they will creep into an hive prepared for that purpose, if it be let before them. We rather, that they may not perish, advise that such things, as we shall hereafter prescribe, be given to the hives when they are sick : for either the kernels of the pomegranate bruised, and sprinkled with Aminean wine, or raisins of the Sun bruised in a mortar with ros Syriacus (Syrian sumach) in equal quantity, and well soaked in rough wine, ought to be given them; or, if these by themselves have no effect, all these same things, an equal weight of each, being smoothed, and reduced into one mass, and boiled with Aminean wine in an earthen vessel, and afterward cooled, ought to be set before them in wooden troughs.

Some people make a decoction of rosemary and mead, and, after it is turned to a jelly, pour it into hollow tiles, and give it them to sip.

Some set ox's or human urine by the hives (as Hyginus affirms). Likewise that disease also is very remarkable, which consumes them, and makes them shrink, and become illfavoured; when some of them frequently carry out of their houses the bodies of those that are dead, and others of them fit dull and languishing within their houses, in sorrowful silence, as in a public mourning. When this happens, food poured into pipes, or troughs made of reeds, is offered to them with well-boiled honey, and smashed oak gall, or dry rose. It is proper also to burn galbanum, that they may be cured with the smell of it; and, when they are wearied, to sustain them with raisins of the Sun, and old soaked must: nevertheless the root of amellus, of which the stalk and sprigs are yellowish, and the flower purple-coloured, does exceeding well; it is boiled with Aminean wine, and strained, and so the dissolved juice of it is given them.

Hyginus indeed, in the book he wrote of bees, says, that Aristomachus was of opinion, that relief ought to be given to such of them as are sick, in this manner: first, That all the vitiated honey-combs be taken away, and fresh food placed anew for them ; and then that they be fumigated. He also thinks, that it does good to bees, wasted with old age, to add a new swarm to them, altho' they may be in danger of being consumed by sedition ; nevertheless they will be glad when a multitude is joined to them.. But, that they may live together in concord, the Kings of those bees, which are translated from another habitation, being, as it were, a foreign people, ought to be removed out of the way. Nevertheless there is no doubt, but that the honeycombs of very numerous swarms, which have young ones already formed in them, ought to be translated, and subjected to those swarms which are fewer in number, that so their houses may be confirmed and established by the adoption, as it were, of a new offspring. But, whenever this shall be done, we must be mindful to put those honeycombs under their care, whose young bees do already break open the places of their abode, and gnaw through the wax which was laid over them as covers to their holes, putting out their heads: for, if we translate the honey-combs while the brood is not come to maturity, the young bees will die, when they cease to be cherished and kept warm.

On many occasions bees also die of a disease, which the Greeks call φαγέδαινα : forasmuch as this is an ordinary custom with bees, to make as much wax-work at first as they think they shall be able to fill up; it sometimes comes to pass, that, after their wax-works are finished, the swarm, wandering at too great a distance, in order to search for honey, is overwhelmed with hidden showers, or whirlwinds, in the woods, and loses the greatest part of the Plebeians: whenever this happens, the few that remain are not able to fill up the honeycombs ; then those parts of the wax-works which are empty rot, and diseases creeping in little by little, after the honey is corrupted, the bees themselves perish also. To prevent this, two different people ought to be united, which may be able to fill up the wax-works while they are yet found ; or, if we have not another swarm fit for our purpose, we must, with a very sharp knife, free the honey-combs from the empty parts before they begin to rot: for this also is of very great importance, that the iron tool be not very blunt, left, being pressed in with greater force, (because it does not easily penetrate) it move the honey-combs out of their places ; for, if this be done, the bees forsake their habitation.

There is this cause also of their destruction, that sometimes for several years following very many flowers come up, and the bees are more intent upon making honey than upon brooding. Therefore some who have less knowledge in these things, are delighted with a great produce, not knowing that the bees are upon the very brink of destruction ; because, being wearied with too much labour, very many of them perish; and their numbers not being increased with new supplies of youth, at last the rest die also. Therefore, if such a spring should happen, that both the meadows and the corn-lands should abound in flowers, it will be of very great advantage, that all the passages of the hives, through which the bees go out, be shut up, leaving small holes, through which they may not be able to go out, that so being withdrawn from their business of making honey, because they have no hopes of filling up all their wax-works with liquors, they may fill them up with a young breed. And these are ordinarily the remedies of swarms of bees that labour under any disease.

WHAT BEES DO & WHAT THEIR KEEPER OUGHT TO DO

Here follows next the care that is to be taken of them through the whole year, as the same Hyginus has described it, in a very easy and agreeable manner. From the first equinox, which happens about the twenty-fourth of March, in the eighth part of Aries, to the rising of the Pleiades, there are reckoned forty-eight days of spring-time. He says, that the bees ought to be cured, for the first time, by opening their hives,, that all the filth and nastiness, which has been gathered during the winter, may be taken out of them ; and that after the spiders, which spoil the honey-combs, are pulled out, the smoke, made by kindling of ox's dung, may be conveyed into them ; for this smoke, from a certain cognation or sameness of parentage and extraction as it were, is very suitable and proper for bees. The little worms also, which are called moths , and the butterflies, must be killed : which pests, adhering for the most part to the honey-combs, fall down from them, if you mix ox's marrow with the dung, and, having set them on fire, convey their burning smell to them : by this management, during the time which we have mentioned, the swarms will be strengthened, and they will, with more courage and resolution, apply themselves to their business, and carry on their works.

But he who has the charge of them, and who nourishes the bees, must be exceeding careful, when he is going to handle the hives, that the day before he be chaste, and pure from all venereal affairs; and, that he neither come to them when he is drunk, nor till such time as he has washed himself; and that he abstain almost from all eatables of a strong disagreeable smell, such as salt-fish or flesh, and all manner of pickle or gravy belonging to them: as also from garlic, onions, and other such-like things, of stinking, acrimonious qualities.

On the forty-eighth day from the vernal equinox, when the Pleiades arise about the eighth day of May, the swarms begin to increase, both in strength and number: but, on the same days also, such swarms as have few and sick bees utterly perish ; and, at the same time, are generated, in the extremities of the honey-combs, young ones of a larger size than those of other bees are ; and some think, that they are Kings. But some of the Greeks call them οἴστρους *(horsefly)*, because they vex and molest the swarms, and do not suffer them to rest: therefore they command them to be killed.

From the rising of the Pleiades to the solstice, which falls in the latter end of the month of June , about the eighth part of Cancer, for the mod part, the hives begin to swarm; at which time they ought to be watched very narrowly, left the young offspring make their escape : and then, from the time that the solstice is past, till the rising of the Dog-star, which are almost thirty days, the corns and the honey-combs are cut down together. But, after what manner these ought to be taken away, we shall afterwards direct, when we come to give directions concerning the making of honey.

But Democritus , and Mago, and Virgil also, have reported, that bees may, at this same time, be generated or produced from a slain bullock. Mago indeed affirms, that the same may be also done from the bellies of oxen; which method of production I think it needless to prosecute more carefully, being of the same mind with Celsus , who says very prudently, that this sort of cattle is never lost with so great a destruction, as to make it necessary to seek to recover them in such a manner. But during this time, and always till the autumnal equinox, the hives must be opened, and fumigated, every tenth day ; which, though it be troublesome to the hives, yet it is agreed, that it is exceeding wholesome. Then you must cool and refresh the bees after they have been fumigated, and are all in an heat, by sprinkling the empty parts of the hives, and pouring the coldest new-drawn water into them: then, if there be any thing that cannot be washed away, it must be cleaned with the pinions of an eagle, or of any other huge fowl also, which have a stiffness in them.

Moreover you must take care, that, if any moths appear, they be swept out of the hives; and that the butterflies be killed, which commonly, abiding among the hives, are destructive to the bees: for they both gnaw into and consume the wax, and with their dung breed worms, which we call hive-moths. Therefore, at the time when the mallows blossom, when there is the greatest multitude of these butterflies, if an high brazen vessel, with a narrow neck like the mile-column, be placed in the evening among the bee-hives, and some light put down to the bottom of it, the butterflies gather together to it from all places ; and, while they flutter about the small flame, they are scorched, because they can neither fly easily upward out of the narrow place, nor, on the other hand, can they retire at a greater distance from the fire, since they are surrounded by the sides of the brazen vessel: therefore they are consumed by the burning heat that is near them. Almost after the fiftieth day from the rising of the Dog-star, Arcturus rose, when the bees make their honeys from the dewy flowers of thyme, and Italian and Greek satury ; and this honey, which is of the best sort, appears in all its lustre and beauty at the autumnal equinox, which is before the first of October, when the Sun is just arrived at the eighth part of Libra. But great care must be taken, between the rising of the Dog-star, and that of Arcturus, that the bees be not surprised and intercepted by the fury and violence of wasps, which, for the most part, lie in wait before the doors of the hives, and watch for their coming out.

After the rising of Arcturus, about the time of the equinox, when the Sun is in Libra , (as I said) is the second taking out of the honeycombs. Then from the time of the equinox, which falls about the twenty-fourth of September, to the setting of the Pleiades , for the space of forty days, the bees lay up for their winter provision the honeys they have gathered from tamarisk-flowers, and shrubs which grow in thickets and woods; from which nothing at all must be taken away, left, being disheartened by repeated injuries, they should, through despair, as it were, of retrieving their affairs, run away, and forsake all.

From the setting of the Pleiades to the winter solstice, which happens almost about the twenty-third of December , in the eighth part of Capricorn, the hives then make use of the honey which they laid up in store, and with it they are nourished and supported till the rising of Arcturus. Nor am I ignorant of Hipparchus's, computation, which teaches, that the solstices and the equinoxes do not happen in the eighth, but in the first parts of the signs. But, in this rural discipline, I now follow the calendars of Eudoxus and Meton, and those of the ancient Astronomers, which are adapted to the public sacrifices; because farmers are both better acquainted with that old opinion which has been commonly entertained : nor, yet, is the niceness and exactness of Hipparchus necessary, to the apprehensions and scanty learning, of farmers. Therefore, at the first setting of the Pleiades , it will be proper to open the hives presently, and to cleanse them from all manner of filth and uncleanness, and to cure them the more carefully, because in the winter-time it is not expedient to move, or lay open, the vases: for which reason, while there is yet any part of the autumn remaining, after you have cleansed their home in a very bright sun-shining day, the covers must be put in the inside, close to the honeycombs, all the empty part of their place being excluded, that so, their cages being reduced to a narrower compass, they may the more easily gather heat during the winter. And this must always be done, even in those hives, which, by reason of the fewness of the common people, are but thinly inhabited.

Moreover, whatever chinks or holes there are in them, we must daub them on the outside with clay and ox's dung mixed together, and leave nothing but the entries for them to go out and come in by. And, although the vases be protected by a portico, nevertheless we must cover them over with straw and leaves put close together, and secure them from cold and storms, as much as the thing will bear. Some kill fowls, and, after they have taken out their entrails, shut them up in the hives; and they afford a gentle heat to the bees, which lurk in their feathers in the winter-time: as also, if their provisions are spent, they feed commodiously upon them when they are hungry, and leave nothing but their bones. But, if the honey-combs are sufficient for them, the fowls remain entire ; nor do they offend the bees with their smell, although they love cleanliness exceedingly. Nevertheless we think it better, in the winter-time, when they are in distress with hunger, to give them, in little troughs at the very entry of their hives, either dry figs bruised and moistened in water, or boiled down grape must to half of the original volume or raisin wine with which liquors you must moisten and imbue clean wool, that the bees, handing upon it, may draw up the juice, as it were, through a siphon. It will also be very proper to give them raisins of the sun, sprinkled a little with water, after we have broken them. And with these sorts of food they must be supported, not only in winter, but also at such times (as I said before) as the spurge, and also the elm-trees, blossom.

After the shortest day of winter is past, they consume almost, in forty days, all the honey that was laid up in store for them (unless a more liberal allowance was left them by their Overseer); and often also, after they have emptied their wax-works, they lie in the honeycombs fasting, and benumbed, without motion, in the manner of serpents, till the rising of Arcturus which is about the thirteenth of February , and by their rest preserve their life : nevertheless, that they may not lose it, if a longer famine assaults them, it is best to put into the hives, through the entrance of the porch, sweet juices or jellies in tubes, and so sustain them during the scarcity of the times, till the rising of Arcturus and the coming of the swallow, promise that the ensuing weather will be more favourable. Therefore after that time, when the cheerfulness of the day permits, they have the courage to go out to the pastures: for after the vernal Equinox, without any delay, they wander up and down everywhere, and pluck the flowers that are fit for the production of their young ones, and carry them home to their houses.

These things Hyginus commands to be most carefully observed through all the seasons of the year: but Celsus adds to them the following things, that few places have the happiness of being in a condition to afford one sort of food for bees in winter, and another in summer ; therefore he denies, that, in those places where flowers, that are proper for them, fail, after the spring of the year is part, the hives ought to be left without moving them ; but that, after the vernal pastures are consumed, they ought to be translated into those places which can nourish the bees more liberally with the rather late flowers of thyme, bastard marjoram, and Greek savory, which, he says, is practised both in the regions of Achaia , where they are translated into the Attican pastures, and in Eubœa, and the Cyclad islands, where they are transported out of the other islands into Scyrus, as also in Sicily, when they are brought to Hybla out of other parts of the country. The same author says, that the wax-works are make of flowers, and the honey of the morning dew, which assumes so much the better quality, the sweeter the materials are, of which the wax is compounded. But he directs us to look carefully into the hives, before they are removed from one place to another and to take out the honey-combs that are old, and full of moths, and ready to drop down; and to reserve only a few of them, and of the best sort, that so as many of them as can be, may be made, at the same time, of the best flowers ; and that such vases as any one has a mind to remove, be carried only in the night-time, and without shaking them.

MAKING OF HONEY, AND WHEN TO PURGE THE HIVES

Presently after the spring is past, follows, as I said, the time for gathering in and making the honey; for which the labour of the whole year is employed. We understand, that the honey is ripe for gathering, when we observe the bees expelling and driving away the drones, which is a kind of animal of a larger growth, and very like a bee, and, as Virgil says, an idle sluggish cattle , and, that fits constantly by the honeycombs, without any industry : for they do not gather any provisions themselves, and consume those that are brought in by others. Nevertheless these drones seem to contribute something towards the procreation of the young generation, they fitting upon those feeds, of which the bees are formed : therefore they are admitted into greater familiarity, in order to hatch, cherish, and educate the new offspring ; but, after the young bees are hatched, they are thrust out of the houses by force, and, as the same poet says, driven from the troughs . Some order them to be entirely exterminated ; but I am of Mago's opinion, and think that this ought not to be done, but that bounds ought to be set to cruelty ; for the whole race ought not to be utterly destroyed, lest the bees be infected with sloth and idleness, which, when the drones consume a part of their provisions, become more nimble and active in repairing their losses: nor, on the other hand, must we suffer a multitude of robbers to grow strong, and form themselves into a body, lest they pillage and destroy all the wealth and riches belonging to others. Therefore, when you see the bees and the drones frequently quarrelling with one another, you must open the hives, and look into them, that if the honeycombs be half-full, they may be deferred, and let alone, for some time ; or, if they are already full of liquor, and all daubed over with wax, as it were, with covers placed upon them, they may be cut down.

But we must seize upon almost the morning of the day for purging the hives; for, it is not proper that the bees, which are already exasperated, should be provoked in the middle of the heat of the day. Two iron-tools are necessary for this use, made of the measure of one foot and an half, or a little larger ; of which, let one be an oblong knife, with a broad edge on both sides, having a crooked scraper or bill for paring on one side ; let the other be plain, and very sharp on the forepart; that by this the honeycombs may be the better cut down, and by that other scraped off; and whatever filth falls down from them, may be drawn towards you : but where the bee-hive has no open porch on the backside, we must convey into it smoke made with galbanum, or dry dung. Moreover, these you must put up into an earthen vessel, mixed with live-coals; and this vessel is made with handles, and shaped like a strait narrow pot, so as one part of it may be sharper, or draw towards a point, by which the smoke may issue out at a small hole ; the other part broader, and with a wide mouth, by which the coals may be blown. When such a pot is applied to the hive, by blowing into it, the smoke is conveyed to the bees, which, not being able to endure the burning smell, presently betake themselves to the forepart of their home, and sometimes retire without the porch.

And, when you have made way for looking more freely into the hives, if there be two swarms of bees, for the most part there are also two kinds of honey-combs found in them; for, even when they live in concord together, each commonalty observes its own custom and manner of shaping and fashioning their wax-works. But all honey-combs do always hang down from the roofs of the hives, and adhering a very little to the sides, so as not to touch the bottom, because that affords a way for the swarms to go and come by. But the figure of the wax-works is such as the shape or make of the hive is ; for both the square and round spaces, and also such as are long, give their own shape, as if they were certain moulds, to the honey-combs; therefore the honey-combs are not always found of the same figure. But, whatever form they may be of, let them not be all taken out: for, at the gathering of the first crop, while the fields do yet abound in pasture, the fifth part of them must be left; and, at the latter crop, when now we are under apprehensions of the winter, the third part must be left. And, yet, this is not a certain measure in all countries ; because due regard must be had for the bees, and provision left for them, in proportion to the multitude of flowers, and the plenty of food, they have. But, if the dependent wax-works run out in length, the honeycombs must be cut with that iron-tool, which is like to a knife; and then they must be received by putting your two arms under them, and so brought out: but, if they run crosswise, and stick to the roofs of the hives, then there is occasion for the iron-tool, made with the paring-knife on the side of it, that, thrusting it into them, they may be cut down with the forepart of the tool turned towards you. But such of them as are old, or spoiled, ought to be taken out, and those that are the soundest, and full of honey, left ; and, finally, if there be any of them that contain young bees, that they be reserved, in order to form a new swarm.

Then your whole store of honey-combs must be brought together into that place, wherein you resolve to make the honey ; and the holes of the walls and windows must be carefully daubed over, and filled up, that there may be no place for the bees to pass through, which eagerly search after their lost goods, as it were, and, having traced them, and found them out, consume them: therefore a smoke must be made, of the same materials, in the entrance of the place also, which may repel such of them as attempt to come in. Then, if any of the hives, that are purged, shall have honey-combs that lie cross the entry, they must be turned, that so the hinder-parts may, by turns, becomes the porches or entries: for so the next time they are purged, the old honey-combs shall rather be taken away than the new, and the wax-works will be renewed, which by how much the older, by so much the worse they are. But if peradventure the hives are surrounded, and inclosed with a wall, and are immoveable, we must take care, that they be purged at one time in the hinder-part, and in the forepart at another time : and this ought to be done before the fifth hour of the day, and then repeated, either after the ninth hour, or the morning following.

But how many honeycombs soever are cut down, it is proper to make the honey the same day, while they are warm. A willow basket, or a sack woven pretty thin with osiers, like an inverted cone, such as that wherewith wine is racked or strained, is hung up in a dark place ; then the honeycombs are gathered into it one by one, as they are taken out. But care must be taken, that those parts of their wax-works, which either have young bees, or red sordid matter in them, be separated from them : for they are of a bad taste, and spoil the honey with their juice. Then, when the strained honey has flowed into a tub set under it to receive it, it is transferred into earthen vessels, which are left open for a few days, till the new honey leave off fermenting; and it must be frequently scummed with a ladle or scummer. Then presently afterwards the fragments of honeycombs, which have remained in the sack, are dressed and handled afresh, and the juice squeezed out of them ; and the honey that flows from them is of a secondary sort, and, by persons that are more exact and careful in their affairs, is laid up apart by itself, lest that which is of the most exquisite taste, by adding this to it, should become worse.

THE MAKING OF WAX

The crop of wax, though it amounts to very little money, is nevertheless not to be neglected, inasmuch as the use of it is necessary for many things. The remains of the honeycombs, when the honey is squeezed out of them, after they are carefully washed with sweet water, are thrown all together into a brazen vessel: then water being put to them, they are melted upon a good fire: and, when this is done, the wax is poured out, and strained through straw or rushes, and then boiled over-again in the same manner as before, and poured out into such moulds as every one thinks most proper, water being first put into them : and it is easy to take it out of the moulds after it is congealed and hardened, because the moisture that is under it does not suffer it to stick to the moulds.

CHAPTER III

BEES IN VARRO'S

ON AGRICULTURE

"It remains now," said Appius, "to rehearse the third and last act of our drama of the husbandry of the steading and to discuss the keeping of fishes."

"The third, indeed," exclaimed Axius, "shall we deprive ourselves of honey because in your youth you never drank mead in your own house, such was your practice of frugality?"

"He speaks the truth," said Appius, to us, "for I was indeed left a poor orphan with two brothers and two sisters to provide for, and it was not until I had married one of them to Lucullus without portion and he had named me his heir that I began to drink mead in my own house and to supply it to my household: but there never was a day when I did not offer it to all my guests. But apart from that, it has been my fortune, not yours , Axius, to have known these winged creatures whom nature has endowed so richly with industry and art, and that you may appreciate that I know more than you do of their almost incredible natural art, listen to what I am to say. It will then be for Merula to develop the practice of the bee keeper, or, as the Greeks call it, μελιττουργία, as methodically as he has his other subjects.

To begin then, bees are generated partly by other bees and partly from the decaying carcass of an ox: so Archelaus in one of his epigrams calls them

' flitting offspring of decaying beef,'
and else where he says,

' wasps spring from horses, bees from calves.'

Bees are not of a solitary habit like eagles, but are of a social nature, like men, a characteristic they share with daws, but not for the same reason, for bees live in colonies, the better to work and build, while daws congregate for gossip. Thus the life of a bee is one of intelligence and art, for man has learned from them to manufacture, to build, and to store his food : three occupations which are not the same but are diverse in their nature, for it is one thing to provide food, another to manufacture wax and honey, and still another to build a house. Has not each cell in a honey comb six sides, or as many as a bee has feet, the art of which arrangement appears in the teaching of the geometricians that of all polygons the hexagon covers the largest area within a circle. Bees feed out of doors, but it is at home that they manufacture that which is the sweetest of all things, acceptable to gods and men alike: for honey comb is offered on the altars and honey is served at the beginning of a dinner and again at dessert.

Bees have institutions like our own, consisting of royalty, government and organized society. Cleanliness in all things is their aim: and so they never alight in any place where there is filth or an evil odour, or even where there is a strong savour of such an unguent as we may consider agreeable. For the same reason if one who approaches them is covered with perfume, they do not lick him as flies do, but they sting him, and by the same token no one ever sees bees crawling on meat and blood and grease, as flies do. And so they only settle in places of sweet savour. They do a minimum of damage because in their harvesting they leave what they touch none the worse. They are not so cowardly as not to resist who ever attempts to disturb them, and yet they are fully conscious of their own weakness. They are called the Winged Servants of the Muses, because when they swarm they are quickly brought together by the music of cymbals and the clapping of hands: and as men assign Helicon and Olympus to be the haunts of the Muses, so nature has attributed the flowery and uncultivated mountains to the bees. They follow their king wheresoever he goes, supporting him when he is tired and even taking him upon their backs if he is unable to fly, so do they wish to serve him. As they are not idlers themselves, so do they hate those who are, and thus driving out the drones, they exclude them from the hive, because they are of no service but merely consume honey: and it happens that a few bees, buzzing with wrath, will drive out a number of drones.

They smear every thing about the entrance to the hive with a gum which is found between the cells which the Greeks call ἐριθάκη. They live under the discipline of an army, taking turns in resting and all doing their equal share of work, and they send out colonies and carry out the orders of their leaders, given with the voice, but as it were with a trumpet: and in like manner they have signs of peace and of war.

But, Merula, now in my course I pass on the torch to you, as our Axius here is doubtless languishing while he has listened to all this natural history, for I have said nothing of profit."

"I do not know," said Merula, " whether what I can say on the subject of the profit to be derived from bees will satisfy you, Axius, but I have as my authorities not only Seius, who takes five thousand pounds of honey every year from the hives he leases, but also our friend Varro here, for I have heard him tell of two brothers Veiani, from the Falerian territory, whom he had under his command in Spain and who, although their father left them only a small house with a curtilage of not exceeding a jugerum in extent, nevertheless made themselves rich. They set bee hives all about the house and planted part of the land in a garden and filled up the rest with thyme and clover and that bee plant known to us as apiastrum , though some call it μελίφυλλον, others μελλισσόφυλλον and still others melittœna: and by this means they were wont to derive, as they estimated, an average income of not less than ten thousand sesterces per annum from honey; but they did this by being willing to wait until they could sell at their own time and price rather than by forcing the market."

"Tell me," exclaimed Axius, "where and how I should establish a bee-stand to make such a handsome profit."

"The apiary," replied Merula, "which some call by the Greek names μελιττών and μελιττοτροφεῖον, and others mellarium, should preferably be placed near the house in a location where there is no echo (for such sounds are deemed to put them to flight, as timid men are by the din of a battle) and where the temperature is mild, exposed neither to the heat of summer nor the cold of winter, giving preferably to the Southeast and near of access to places where their food is abundant and there is a supply of fresh water. If there is no natural supply of food available you should plant such things as best serve bees for pasture, namely: roses, thyme, bee balm, poppies, beans, lentils, peas, basil, gladiolus, alfalfa, and especially clover which is of great service to the bees which are sick, for it begins to bloom at the vernal equinox and lasts until that of autumn. As clover is the best food for sick bees, so thyme is the best for making honey, and it is because Sicily abounds in good thyme that it takes the palm for producing honey. On this account some men bruise thyme in a mortar and mix warm water with it and then spray all their nursery plants with it for the sake of the bees.

The hives should be set as near the house as convenient: some men even put them under the very portico for greater safety. Hives are made in various shapes and sizes and of different material; thus some make them round out of wicker work: others of frame covered with bark: others use hollow tree trunks: others vessels of pottery: some even build them square out of rods, allowing about three feet in length and a foot in height, but these dimensions should be reduced where you have not enough bees to fill a hive of that size, for fear that the bees might become discouraged by too large an empty space.

The bee hive derives its name alvus , which is the same as our word for belly, from the fact that it holds food, that is to say, honey; and it is on this analogy that hives are usually shaped to imitate the form of the belly, small in the waist and bulging out below. When the hives are made of wicker work they should be coated evenly within and without with ox dung so that the bees may not be driven away by the roughness of their roof. The hives should be so ordered under the shelter of a wall that they may not be disturbed nor touch one another when arranged in ranks, for it is the practice to place hives in two and some times three separated ranks, but the opinion is that it is better to reduce the ranks to two than to increase them to four. In the middle of the hive small openings are made on the right and the left to serve as entrances for the bees, and on top is placed a practicable cover, which may be removed to give access to the honey comb. This is best when made of bark, and worst of pottery, because that is strongly affected both by the cold of winter and the heat of summer. In spring and summer the bee keeper should inspect each hive at least three times a month, fumigating them lightly, cleaning and throwing out dirt and worms. At the same time he should take precautions to keep down the number of princes, for they keep the bees from work by stirring up sedition. There are said to be three kinds of royalties among the bees: the black, the red and the mottled, or, as Menecrates writes, two: the black and the mottled: and as the latter is the better it behooves the bee keeper, when he finds both kinds in a hive, to kill the black one, as he is forever playing politics against the other king, whereby the hive must suffer, for inevitably one of the kings will flee or be driven out, in either case taking his party with him.

Of working bees the small round mottled variety is considered the best. The drone, or, as some call him, the thief, is black with a large belly. The wasp, which has some resemblance to a bee, is not, however, a fellow labourer, but attacks the bees with his sting, wherefore the bees keep him at a distance.

Bees are themselves distinguished as wild and tame. I call those wild which feed in the forests, and those tame which feed in cultivated places. The forest bees are smaller in size and hairy but better workmen.

In buying bees it behooves the purchaser to see whether they are well or ailing. The signs of health are a thick swarm, well groomed appearance and a hive being filled in a workmanlike manner. The signs of lack of condition on the other hand are a hairy and bristling appearance and a dusty coat, unless this last is caused by a pressure of work, for under such circumstances they often wear themselves down and become thin.

If the hives are to be transferred from one place to another it is necessary to choose a fit time to make the move and a suitable place to receive them. As to time, spring is preferable to winter because in winter they have difficulty in adjusting themselves to a new location and so often run away, as they do also if you move them from a good location to a place where proper pasture is not available. Nor is a transfer from one hive to another in the same place to be undertaken carelessly, but that to which the bees are to be transferred should be rubbed with bee balm, which will serve as a bait for them, and some pieces of honey comb should be placed in it, not far from the entrances, for fear that the bees might run away if they found the larder of their new home empty.

Menecrates says that bees contract a malady of the bowels from their first spring pasture on the blossoms of the almond and the cornel cherry and are cured by giving them urine to drink.

That gummy substance which the bees use, chiefly in summer to construct a sort of curtain between the entrance and the hive, is called propolis , and by the same name is used by physicians in making plasters: by reason of which use it sells in the Via Sacra for more than honey itself. That substance which is called erithacen , and is used to glue the cells together, is different from both honey and propolis: it is supposed to have a quality of attraction for bees and is accordingly mixed with bee balm and smeared on the branch or other place on which it is desired to have a swarm light. The comb is made of wax and is multicellular, each cell in it having six sides or as many as nature has given the bee feet. It is said that bees do not gather from the same plants all the materials which enter in these four substances which they manufacture, namely: propolis, erithacen, wax and honey. Thus from the pomegranate and the asparagus they gather food alone, wax from the olive tree, honey from the fig, but not of good quality: other plants like the bean, the bee balm, the gourd and the cabbage serve a double purpose and yield both wax and food: while the apple and the wild pear serve a similar double purpose but for food and honey and the poppy again for wax and honey.

Others again provide material for three purposes, food, honey and wax, such as the almond and the charlock. In like manner there are flowers from each of which they derive a different one of these substances, and others from which they derive several of them: while they make distinctions in respect of plants according to the quality of the product they yield, — or rather the plants make the distinction for them — as with respect to honey, some yield liquid honey, like the skirwort, and others thick honey like the rosemary. So again honey of insipid flavour is made from the fig, good honey from clover, and the best of all from thyme.

And since drink is part of a bee's diet and water is the liquid they use, there should be provided near the stand a place for them to drink, which may be either a running stream or a reservoir not more than two or three fingers deep in which bricks or stones are placed in such a way as to project a little from the water, and so furnish a place for the bees to sit and drink; but the greatest care must be taken to keep this water fresh, as it is of high importance to the making of good honey.

As the bees cannot go out to distant pasture in all weathers, food must be prepared for them, as otherwise they will live on their supply of honey and so deplete the store in the hive. For this purpose ten pounds of ripe figs may be boiled in six congii of water and bits of the paste thus prepared should be set out near the hives. Others provide honey water in little dishes and float flocks of clean wool on them through which the bees may suck without risk of either getting more than is good for them or of being drowned. One such dish should be provided for each hive and they should be kept filled. Others again bray dried grapes and figs together and, mixing in some boiled must, make a paste of which bits are exposed near the hives during such part of the winter as the bees are still able to go forth in search of food.

When a swarm is about to come out of the hive (which happens when a number of young bees have matured, and the hive determines to send their youth out to found a colony, as formerly the Sabines often were compelled to do on account of the number of their children) there are two signs by which the intention may be known: one that for several days before hand, and especially in the evening, many bees weave themselves together and hang upon the entrance of the hive like grapes : the other that when they are about to go forth or have already begun to go they buzz together lustily, as soldiers do when they break camp. Those who have come forth first fly about the hive waiting for the others, who have not yet collected, to join them. When the bee keeper notices this he has only to throw dust on them and at the same time beat upon some copper vessel to collect them, thoroughly frightened, where he desires in some nearby place on which he has smeared erithacen and bees' balm and other things in which they delight. When they have settled down he should place near them a hive smeared within with the same baits, and then, by blowing a light smoke around them, compel them to enter the hive. When thus introduced into their new abode the swarm makes itself at home cheerfully, so that even if placed next to the parent hive they will prefer their new colonial settlement.

And now, having told you all I know about the care of bees, I will speak of that for which the industry is carried on, that is to say, of the profit.

The honey is taken off when the hive is full, as may be determined by removing the cover of the hive, for if the openings of the combs are seen to be sealed, as it were with a skin, then the hive is full of honey: but the bees themselves give notice of this condition by keeping up a loud buzzing within, by their agitation when they go in and out and by driving out the drones.

In taking off honey some say that you should be content with nine parts, leaving the tenth, because if you take it all the bees will desert the hive : others leave a still larger proportion than I have mentioned.

As those who crop their corn land every year obtain good yields only at intervals, so it is with bee hives : you will have more industrious and more profitable bees if you do not exact of them the same tribute every year.

It is considered that honey should be taken off for the first time at the rising of the Pleiades, for the second time at the end of summer before Arcturus has reached the zenith, and for the third time after the setting of the Pleiades, but this last time beware not to take more than one-third of the store even if the hive is full, leaving the other two-thirds for the winter supply, but if the hive is only partially filled nothing should be taken off. In any event, when a large amount of honey is to be taken off a hive it should not be done all at once or ostentatiously less the bees be discouraged. Those combs which, on being taken off, are found to be partly unfilled with honey or to be soiled, should be pared with a knife.

Care must be taken that the weaker bees in a hive are not oppressed by the stronger, for this diminishes the profit: to this end the minority party may be colonized under another king. When bees are given to fighting with one another, you should sprinkle them with honey water, upon which they will not only cease fighting but will crowd together and kiss one another: and this will prove the case even more if they are sprinkled with mead, for the savour of the wine in it will cause them to apply themselves so greedily that they will fuddle themselves in sucking it. If the bees seem lazy about coming out to work and any part of them get the habit of remaining in the hive, they should be fumigated and odoriferous herbs, like bees' balm and thyme, should be placed near the hive. Watchful care is necessary to protect them from ruin by heat or cold. If the bees are overtaken by a sudden rain or cold while at pasture (which rarely happens for they usually foresee such things) and are stricken down by the heavy rain drops and laid low and stunned, you should gather them in a dish and place them under cover in a warm place until the weather has cleared, when they should be sprinkled with ashes of fig wood (making sure that the ashes are rather hot than warm) the dish should then be shaken gently without touching the bees with your hand, and placed in the sun.

When the bees feel this warmth they revive and get on their feet again, just as flies do after they have been apparently drowned. This should be done near the hive so that when the bees have come to themselves they may return home and to work."

CHAPTER IV

BEES IN VIRGIL'S

THE GEORGICS

Of honey, wind-bred bounty of the sky,
Next let me sing. And to the humble task
Once more, Maecenas, lend a gracious ear!
A pageant wonderful to thee I show.
The story of a people light as air.
Their large-souled leaders, and of all their kind
The customs, occupations, kingdoms, wars.
A task of narrow span, but no small praise,
If unpropitious powers bar not my way.
And favoring Phoebus grant a poet's prayer.

First find the bees safe shelter and abode
Where no winds enter, such as backward blow
The honey-bearers from their homeward way;
And where no sheep, no kids with frolic horn,
Trample upon the flowers, nor roving calf
Swish through the dewy grass and tread it down.
Let not the scale-backed, painted lizard peer
Too nigh the bees' full barns, nor thievish birds,
Fly-catchers, or the swallow whose soft breast
By her own murderous hands was dabbled o'er.
For such make forage far and wide and bear
In ruthless beak the insect harvesters
As sweet, winged morsels to their nestlings wild.
But flowing fountains near the hives should be,

Still pools with fresh, green mosses bordered round,
And through the grasses a small rill should run.
Above their portals let a branching palm
Or large wild olive its deep shadows throw,
That when new-chosen chiefs lead forth in Spring
The young swarm, and escaping from their cells
The playful legion greets its native air,
Then the cool bank may lure them to repose
From the hot sun-beam, and the neighboring tree
Its leafy hospitality extend.

In the mid-stream, though slow or swift it run.
Set willow boughs or large, smooth stepping-stones,
To serve for bridges where th' alighting bee
May dry his spread wings in the summer sun.
If, ere he heeded, some impetuous breeze
Have drenched or wrecked him in that little sea.
Around the place let verdant cassias grow,
With much strong-scented thyme, and let the stream
Flow through sweet beds of thirsting violets.
The hives themselves, if stitched of hollow bark
Or plaited basket-work, should have but doors
Of narrow compass, lest in winter's chill
The honey thicken, or in sultry days
Melt and ooze off: for bees make anxious toil
'Gainst either trouble; with no aimless care
They eagerly seal up all crevices,
All air-holes in their walls, filling the cracks
With flowery pollen; they collect and save
Their thick glue for this work, which faster binds
Than bird-lime or the pitch of Phrygian pines.
Often they build a secret hearth and home
By burrowing in the earth, I hear men say;
And hid in hollowed crags their nests are found,
Or deep in cavernous bole of fallen tree.

Thou likewise o'er the bee-hives' crannied sides
Wilt smear warm clay, patting it down, and then
Strew leaves on top. But let no yew-tree grow
Where the bees haunt, nor burn red crabs near by.
Nor let there be deep mud-holes or the stench
Of filthy slough; nor let o'erarching rocks
Be rife with echoes doubling every cry.

Now further counsel. When the golden sun
Bids the defeated winter sink away
Under the earth, and quite unbars the sky
To summer's burning glory, then the bees
Roam over glade and grove, harvesting well
The gorgeous flowers, and sip on lightsome wing
The surface of the streams. From this time forth
They fondly tend, with sweet, mysterious joy.

The young brood in the nests, and skilfully
Sculpture the wax and mould the honey-comb.
At the same season, when the caravan
Pours from the hives and skyward, starward, soars
Along the glowing air, your eyes behold
With wonder how the wind will gather them
In one dark cloud. Then watch them where they move !
For always flowing springs and sheltering trees
They seek for: then take heavy-scented herbs
Bruised balsam and the wax-flower's humble weed.
And sprinkle with their juice some chosen spot
And clash loud cymbals like a Corybant.

At this balm-breathing place the swarm will stay
And rear, as is their wont, the future brood.
But sometimes they declare a war: for oft
Between two kings a fatal strife begins
Tumultuous, and one discerns from far

The anger of the mob, whose hearts leap up
All fury for the fight. A loud alarm
Like hoarse-tongued blare of martial brass
Rebukes the lingerers. A wild cry is heard
In semblance of the trumpet's billowy sound.
Then comes the raging charge: their little wings
Glitter, their stings are sharp as javelins.
They grapple limb with limb, and round each chief,
Each king's pavilion, there is tug of war.
As with fierce war-cry each defies the foe.
In such wise, when some rainless day in Spring
Invites them to the open fields, they burst
Impetuous from their portals, and the bees
Join battle high in air; a mighty din
Arises; they roll up confusedly
In one great globe, then drop they headlong down;
Not thicker is the fall of wind-blown hail
Nor shower of acorns from storm-shaken tree.
The chieftains in the midmost war are known
By their far-shining wings and show abroad
How vast a valor such small breasts contain;
So stubbornly they hold their ground, until
The mightier victor of this host or that
Compels to panic flight his routed foe.
Yet all this stir of passion and fierce fight.

If but a little dust be tossed in air,
Will be subdued, dispersed, and die away.
But when the two chief captains homeward come
From conduct of the war, the vanquished one
Must be condemned to die, lest he should waste
The public substance. Let the victor take
An undisputed throne. One now shines forth
In golden flecked attire; of race diverse
The twain appear, one strong and flourishing.

Of haughty looks and bright with crimson scales,
The other in foul garb inglorious
Drags slothfully his swollen bulk along.
And like their kings their followers also prove
Of differing kind : some foul and colorless
As dust-cloud on a highway, such as chokes
The thirsty traveller; but the others flash
With glittering beams and wear a glow of fire.
Their backs all blazoned with bright drops of gold.
This is the nobler breed; from these when heaven
Brings the due season round thou shalt obtain
Sweet honey, and not only sweet but clear, —
A mellowing mixture if the wine be strong.

But when the swarm flits aimless through the air
Heeds not its honied treasure, and would soar
Free of the cool hives, in such idle play
Thy art must govern their inconstant mind.
The task is easy. Thou hast but to clip
The leaders' wings; for when these lag below
No common bee will soar aloft, nor dare
Give marching orders to the bivouac.
Then gardens with the breath of saffron flowers
Tempt them to linger, where 'gainst birds and thieves
With willow scythe the god of Hellespont,
Priapus, is a faithful sentinel.
Then the bee-keeper from the lofty hills
Must fetch pine boughs and thyme leaves, scattering both
All round the hives; and with his own strong hand
Set out fine, healthy plants, and guide the flow
Of friendly streams to bless his garden ground.
But truly, if I were not reefing sail
Nor ending now a long, laborious voyage.
And were I less in haste to beach my keel,
Perchance I could make venture of a song

On gardens and the skill to make them bloom: —
How Paestum's roses twice a year unfold.
How endives flourish in a trickling rill.
Parsley at brookside green, and rambling gourds
Thrust forth their rounded bellies through the grass.
Then would I of that tardy loiterer tell.
Narcissus, of th' acanthus' nodding stem.
Of ivies pale, and pathways bordered green
With myrtle.
          For beneath Oebalia's towers
Where dark Galaesus flows through golden corn,
I once made friendship of an aged man
From Corycus, who had a few poor roods
Of worthless land. No pasturage was there
For cattle nor for flocks convenient food.
Nor soil for vines. Yet he among its thorns
Raised his small plot of greens and round them sowed
A few white lilies, vervain's sacred leaf,
With poppies of rare savor, while his soul
Vied with the wealth of kings, when late at eve
He heaped th' unpurchased banquet on his board.
The rose of Spring and autumn's apples red
He was the first to pluck. When winter's chill
Still split the rocks with frost and laid cold curb
Upon the frozen stream, already he
Was toying with some soft-tressed hyacinth,
Chiding slow summer and the laggard Spring.
He was, be sure, the first whose brooding bees
Were in full swarm; his fingers earliest
Pressed forth the bubbling honey from the comb.
Lime-trees he planted and luxuriant pines,
And what his fruit trees in the blossoming Spring
Of promise bore, not less rich autumn gave.
His elm-tree saplings even when full-grown
He could transplant, or pear-trees big and strong.

Or the young plane-tree when its spreading boughs
Screened from the sun the guest that drank his wine.
Yet all these joys I lack full space to sing.
Let later singers the sweet story tell.

Come then, give ear, while I those gifts declare
Which bees received of Jove, when for such boon
They, following where the clash of cymbals called
And that wild chant the Cretan priesthood sang,
In Dicte's cave fed heaven's infant king.
They are the only creatures to possess
Offspring in common, and their city build
Of undivided houses, where they live
Obeying mighty laws, and they alone
True fatherland and fixed abodes obtain.
Warned of approaching winter, they employ
Their summer's day in toil, and store their gains
As common treasure. Certain chosen ones
Forage for food and, so it is agreed,
Keep busy in the fields while others pent
Within the walls of houses, firmly mould
The bottom of the comb; for which they use
Narcissus' tear and gums from bark of trees,
Then roof with clinging wax. Others lead forth
Their infant brood in air, the tribe to be.
Still others closely pack the honey-dew,
Till every cell with nectared sweet runs o'er.
For others 'tis th' apportioned task to stand
Gate-sentinels, and keep alternate watch
For auguries of rain and cloudy skies.
These at the gates receive the little loads
Of the home-comers, or lined up for war.
Fight the dull drones and bar them from the hive.
Eager the toil and swift. The honey-comb

Breathes to the air sweet fragrance of wild thyme.

It minds me of the Cyclops' wondrous task,
When from the molten mass of yielding ore
They forge their thunderbolts : a certain part
Force bull's-hide bellows to puff back and forth
The windy blasts; part temper in deep pool
The hissing metal; with their anvil's weight
The floor of Aetna groans; their lifted arms
With power gigantic strike the measured blows.
And with huge pincers gripping on the steel
They roll it round. With not less furious toil,
If such small creatures may with large compare,
The bees upon Hymettus' hill divine
Rush to their labors, mightily compelled
By inborn love of riches, each pursuing
His separate task and gain. The oldest ones
Take counsel for their city, raising walls
About the honied treasure, or build up
Ingenious dwellings; but the younger sort
Come late at eve and weary, bringing home
Thigh-loads of flowery food. They travel far
Feeding on arbute or the silvery bloom
Of willows, or on blushing crocuses.
Or fruitful limes and deep-dyed hyacinth.
But all together seek repose or toil
At the same hours. When morning's ray appears
They hurry from the gates, not one delays.
But when the star of twilight lifts in heaven
Its monitory beam, all homeward fly.
Quitting the forage of the plain, to find
Safe shelter and to ease their wearied limbs.
Loud is the air when the returning swarm
Hums round the hive; but later, when they lie
Each in his chamber, then the silence falls

And shadows of the night, while welcome sleep
Possesses all. But if the opening morn
Show dark and rainy skies, they fly not far
From house and home, nor venture high in air
If tempests threaten, but in safety rove
Close to their city walls, and seek supply
Of water, taking but a brief detour.
Sometimes they lift small pebbles, as light boats
Bear ballast through the waves; and weighted so,
They keep their balanced flight through stormful air.

But veriest marvel of the ways of bees
Is that their limbs mix not in love's embrace
Nor weaken them by lust, nor ever bear
Their young in pangs of travail; but from leaves
Of fragrant herbs the mothers with their lips
Breathe in their offspring, and all virginal
Give birth to kings and tiny citizens,
Repeopling so their waxen state and throne.
Often they wound on flinty rocks their wings
And faithful to their burdens bravely die.
Such zeal they have for flowers, and in their life
Of honey-gathering such sweet glory find.

Thus though each single life has narrow bound,
But seven summers, no more, the race of bees
Lives on immortally. Age after age
Their noble line is blest and counts its roll
Of a long multitude of sires of sires.
But to their kings the fealty they pay
Not Egypt nor the Lydian monarchy
Surpass, not Parthia nor the golden Mede
Beside Hydaspes' wave. For when their king
Securely stands, a common thought and soul
Fills all the host; but if the chieftain fall

All loyal bonds are snapt, and their own rage
Tears down the toil-built honey and destroys
The waxen treasure-house. The king defends
Their work, their wealth; while they his state surround
With honor and applause, and at his side
Attend him in loud-shouting, loyal throng.
They lift him on their shoulders; or in war
Fling their own bodies in his foeman's way,
Seeking by many a wound a glorious death.

These acts and powers observing, some declare
That bees have portion in the mind of God
And life from heaven derive; that God pervades
All lands, the ocean's plain, th' abyss of heaven.
And that from him flocks, cattle, princely men,
All breeds of creatures wild, receive at birth
Each his frail, vital breath; that whence they came
All turn again, dissolving; so that death
Is nowhere found, but vital essences
Upsoaring in the vast, o'er-vaulted sky
Move unextinguished through the starry throng.

If e'er thou wouldst from its small shelf unseal
The honied store, first having purified
Thy lips and breath, with water sprinkle well
And waft the wreathing smoke with wave of hand.
Twice in the year the teeming brood is born,
Two harvests have they : when the Pleiad star
Spurns with her winged feet the ocean's rim,
And when in flight before the stormful sign
Of the great Fish, on journey dark and drear
She sinks from heaven beneath the wintry wave.
This is the season when the wrath of bees
Breaks bound, and if one harm them, they infuse
A venom in each sting and in thy veins

Implant a hidden barb, leaving behind
Their own lives in the little wounds they give.
If a hard winter bodes, and thy fond care
Forecasts their future, pitying what would be
Thy spirit-broken swarm's distressful state.
Fear not to smoke them out with odorous thyme
And cut the empty combs. Haply some newt
Has bored the wax unseen, or in the cells
The sunbeam-fearing beetles throng, or they
Who sit at unearned feasts, the shirking drones.
Or some rude hornet with his mightier sting
Has forced his way, or moth of dreadful breed.
Or spider, by Minerva curst, has hung
Her swinging webs at entrance of the hives.
The more the bees feel poverty, the more
They turn to eager labors and retrieve
A fallen people's fortune, heaping high
Their crowded marts and flowery granaries.

But if it chance, because the life of bees
Has the same ills as ours, that their small frames
Languish in pestilence, these certain signs
Will tell thee of their plight: the stricken ones
Keep changing color and their visages
Are hideously wasted; then the tribe
Bears slowly from its house the lifeless forms
With mournful pomp of death; or clinging close

With interwoven feet they swing aloft
Above their threshold, or with portals barred
Linger within the walls, all spiritless
With hunger and benumbed with shrivelling cold.
Then sounds a deeper voice, a booming note
Ever increasing, as when north winds roar
In wintry woods, or when a roughened sea

Flows moaning from the shore, or when swift fires
Leap, loud and strong behind shut furnace doors.
Burn at such time the sweet-breathed galbanum.
Carry them honey poured in pipes of reed
Tempting them thus to feed and calling them
To the familiar feast. 'Tis also well
To flavor it with sap of powdered galls
And rose-leaves dried, or freshly trodden must
Warmed at a fire, or raisin-clusters plucked
From some choice vineyard; also leaves of thyme.
The Attic sort, and that strong-scented stem
The Centaurs knew. Then there's a useful flower
Growing in meadows, which the country folk
Call star-wort, not a blossom hard to find,
For its large cluster lifts itself in air
Out of one root; its central orb is gold
But it wears petals in a numerous ring
Of glossy purplish blue; 'tis often laid
In twisted garlands at some holy shrine.
Bitter its taste; the shepherds gather it
In valley-pastures where the winding streams
Of Mella flow. The roots of this steeped well
In hot, high-flavored wine, thou may'st set down
At the hive door in baskets heaping full.

But if thy whole swarm at a stroke should fail
With no stock left for breeding, let my song
Tell now a memorable art derived
From an Arcadian king, and show what way
When bulls are slaughtered oftentimes their blood
Out of corruption generates the bee. .
From ancient lore I will the tale unfold.
For where Canopus' favored citizens
Beneath the Macedonian's golden sway
By the full, lingering waters of the Nile,

Sail o'er their farms in painted skiffs (though oft
The Persian bowmen vex the borderland)
And where in seven floods the rushing stream
Divides, and feeds the green Egyptian field
With that rich earth the river downward draws
From where the dark-skinned Aethiopians roam —
Throughout that famous land their opulent ease
Depends upon this art.
                       First they choose out
Some place of narrow bounds, and roofing o'er
With tiles, building around it straitened walls,
They cut four windows open to four winds.
But not square to the sun. Then from the herd
They take a steer, a two-year-old, whose horns
Just curl upon his brows; his nostrils twain
And breathing mouth, though stoutly he resist.
They seal fast; then with rain of many blows
They beat his life out, crushing every part
Except th' unbroken hide. The body then
Is laid in the enclosure; under it
They scatter boughs, the fragrant leaves of thyme
And cassia freshly pulled. This must be done
When first the Spring winds set the waters free,
Before the meadows blush with early flowers
Or ere the chattering swallow hangs her nest
Under the roof-tree beam. Soon waxing warm
The moisture rises in the softened bones,
And living creatures, wonderful to see.
Come forth, at first all footless, but erelong
With whir of wings the restless multitude
In swelling numbers on the liquid air.
Bursts swift away; like some full, pouring shower
From summer cloud, or like the arrowy rain
From a loud, quivering bowstring skyward flung,
When Parthia's light-foot host invites the war.

What god, O Muses, labored to devise
This art for us, or how did human skill
Unto such novel venture find a way ?
The shepherd Aristeaus climbing forth
From Tempe's vale and river, having lost.
So runs the tale, his swarms of bees, and vexed
With fever and with famine, stood all tears
Hard by the sacred source of Peneus' wave,
And making loud complaint and bitter cry.
Called thus: "Cyrene, mother mine, whose home
Is deep below this stream, why bor'st thou me
Of famous, heavenly line (if I may claim
Apollo, lord of Thymbra, for my sire,
As thou hast said) yet gav'st me birth
To be of fate the scorn ? Where hast thou flung
Thy love of me away ? Why bid aspire
To heaven and godhead ? Look, my life as man
Has lost its pride and crown, its busy care
Of field and flock, with many a patient proof,
So painfully achieved. And yet thou wert
My mother ! Therefore come ! Let thine own hand
Spoil and uproot my fruitful orchards fair.
Hurl fire on my folds, my harvest blight.
Burn up my seedlings and with ruthless axe
My vineyards hew away ! — if verily
Such scorn thou hast of all that brings me praise."
Now from her chamber deep below the wave
His mother heard his voice. Her nymphs hard by
Sat in a circle spinning from their looms
Rare fleeces dipped in hues of hyaline :
Ligea, Xantho, with Phyllodoce
And Drymo, o'er whose snowy necks flowed down
Their gleaming hair, Cydippe and gold-tressed
Lycorias, the one a virgin free.
The other to the labors lately come

Of motherhood; there were the sisters twain
Clio and Beroe, ocean's daughters both.
In golden zone and gorgeous mantles clad;
Deiopea, Opis, Ephyre
And fleet-foot Arethusa, who at last
Had laid her arrows by. This sea-nymph throng
Was listening to the tales of Clymene:
Of Vulcan's fruitless caution and the guile
Of amorous Mars that gained him stolen joy;
And of unnumbered loves of gods she told.
Since first the world began. So while their hands
Twirled from the spindles the soft threads of wool.
They heard th' enchanting burden of her song.
But once again upon his mother's ear
Smote Aristaeus' cry, and those sea-nymphs
Listened amazed upon their crystal thrones.
Then Arethusa, ere her sisters spoke,
Uplifting from the wave her golden brow,
Thus called from far: " Cyrene, sister mine,
Hear not in vain that terrifying cry.
Behold thy darling and thy chiefest care.
Unhappy Aristaeus, stands in tears
On brink of Peneus' wave, and on thy name
Calls loud to tell thee of thy cruelty."
Once more the mother with unwonted fear
Trembled at heart: " Oh, hither where we dwell
Show him his way," she said, " Grant him the boon
To cross yon threshold of divine abodes."
Straightway she gave command that far and wide
The opening river floods should yield free path
To the young shepherd's feet. And lo ! the waves
Rose like a hilltop round him and received
In vast embrace, letting the hero pass
Deep down below the river. Now his eyes
Gazed wondering on his goddess-mother's realm.

He passed through watery kingdoms, by dark lakes
All cavern-girdled, by loud-roaring groves.
Then by the noise of mighty floods struck dumb
He saw vast rivers flowing under earth
Each in its region due. The Phasis there
And Lycus he could see, and that first well
Whence breaks to birth Enipeus' stream profound.
There Father Tiber rose, and Anio's
Swift current, rock-bound, echoing Hypanis,
Caicus, Mysia's stream; there golden-horned,
His countenance a bull, Eridanus
That with more fury than all floods beside
Sweeps through rich farms to meet the purple sea.

Soon came the youth beneath the pendent stone
That roofed his mother's halls. Cyrene saw
Her son's unfruitful tears. Her sisters brought,
In order due, ablution for his hands
And napkins of shorn fringe; they piled the board
With feasting and with wine-cups oft refilled.
The sacred altars blazed with fragrant fires.
The mother cried: "Bring forth a brimming bowl
Of Lydian vintage. We make offering
Unto the ocean's god." Wherewith she prayed
To ocean the great parent, and the nymphs:
A hundred haunt the groves, a hundred guard
The rivers, and they are her sisters all.
Three times on Vesta's burning hearth she poured
A stream of wine, three times the vanquished fire
Leaped sparkling to the roof-tree in fresh flame.
The happy omen cheered her fearful mind
And thus she spoke:
                              "In far Carpathian main
The sea-green Proteus dwells, a prophet-bard.
Whose dolphin chariot skims the mighty deep

With yoke of two-foot horses. At this hour
Back to his own Emathian shores he hies.
His fatherland Pallene. We sea-nymphs
And gray-beard Nereus greatly worship him.
For he, prophetic soul, has vision clear
Of all that is and was and soon will be.
The power is Neptune's gift, at whose command
He, under rolling tides, the shepherd is
Of monster flocks and of foul-featured seals.
'Tis he, my son, whom thou must bind with cords
Then will he show what brought thy plagues to pass
And grant escape. No precept will he give
Save on compulsion; thou canst not persuade
By prayers. Take him by violence and bind
Strong fetters round his limbs, until at last
Thou shalt dissolve his vain, deceiving spells.
Myself at noon's full blaze, when all the fields
Are thirsting and the flocks in shadows lie.
Will lead thee where this aged prophet hides
When weary of the sea. Thou, while he sleeps,
Seize on him with firm hand and fetters strong.
His changeful shapes will mock thee; he will wear
The forms of many a beast: he will appear
A bristling boar, a tiger grim, a snake
Of scaly coils, a red-necked lioness;
Or he will seem a sound of crackling fire
And through thy fetters leap, or suddenly
Drop like fast-flowing water from thy grasp.
But thou the more he shifts, the more he flies
From form to form, bind thou the cords, my son.
Yet tighter, till at last thine eyes behold
The self-same shape his changeful body wore
When with closed eyes he first lay down and slept."
She spoke: and round her breathed the fragrant air
Of her immortal nature, which did flow

Over her son's whole body, from his head
His ordered tresses shed an effluence
Divinely sweet, and through his manly limbs
New vigor flowed.
                    A cavern vast
Lies in a certain mountain's hollowed side,
Where driven by the winds the swollen waves
Draw back divided, and where many a time
The storm-caught mariners safe shelter find.
Deep in its gloom behind a barrier stone
Lay Proteus. There the sea-nymph set her son
In shadowy ambush far from light of day,
But she herself, all mantled in a cloud,
Watched at a distance. 'Twas the season when
The fierce Dog Star that burns the fevered Ind
Flamed in the sky, and half the orb of heaven
The fiery sun had passed. The pastures green
Were withered, the dry-throated rivers ran
Emptied, and their warm beds of oozy clay
Lay parching in the sunshine. Proteus then
Out of the billowy seas had sought repose
Within his wonted cavern. Round him ranged
The watery tribes that habit the great sea.
In frolic shaking off the bitter brine
Like showers of dew; far-scattered on the shore
Were stretched the sleeping seals. The god himself
Seemed like the herdsman in the hills, what time
The evening star leads back from field to fold
His cattle and his flock; his bleating lambs
Tempt the far-listening wolves — he takes his place
On some tall stone and counts them as they pass.
Now Aristaeus, his occasion come,
Soon as the old man's weary limbs took rest,
Rushed in upon him with a mighty cry
And bound him as he lay. The struggling god

Forgot not his own arts, and changed himself
Into all wondrous things : to flames of fire,
To frightful monsters and swift-passing streams.
But when for all his guile he could not flee,
Yielding, he took his own true shape, and spake
From human lips this answer: "At whose word,
Com'st thou my dwelling nigh, presumptuous boy ."
What wouldst thou have ? " The other answered him:
"Thou knowest, Proteus, knowest all untold.
What scapes thy knowledge ? Prithee now give o'er!
By word divine I come, and ask of thee
Some oracle to help my desperate need."

He ceased. At last the prophet overborne
By much constraint, rolled wide his blazing eyes
And glances dark, gnashed terribly his teeth
And from his lips the words of fate set free.
"None less than wrathful god pursues thee thus.
For dire offences is thy suffering paid.
'Tis Orpheus, woe-begone, but guiltless all,
Sends thee his vengeance until fate oppose;
For mighty is his anger evermore
Robbed of his wife. It was thy chase she fled
Swift through the stream, but saw not in her path
The huge snake hiding on the deep-grassed shore, —
Doomed girl ! The forest-nymphs, her lovely peers,
To the high hilltops sent their wailing cry;
The peaks of Rhodope lamented loud,
Lofty Pangaea, and the land of Thrace
Beloved of Mars; swift Hebrus flowed in tears
And Orithya wept. But he, the bard
Soothed his love-anguish on the concave shell,
Singing of thee, sweet wife, and wandering lone
Upon a desolate shore. Of thee he sang
When morning rose and with departing day.

He entered also at the doors of hell.
At Pluto's vast abode, that clouded grove
Black with eternal horror. He drew near
Those fleshless ghosts and Hades' grisly king,
Whose hearts at human prayers no motion feel.
Yet at his song, from deepest Erebus
The lifeless phantoms and thin shadows came,
Loving and pitiful; like flocks they seemed
Of birds that hide in leafy boughs, when night
Or wintry tempest drives them from the hills.
Mothers and husbands came, with lifeless forms
Of high-souled heroes, boys, unwedded maids.
And youthful manhood given to the tomb
Before fond parents' eyes. Around them flowed
Cocytus, dark with slime and loathly weed.
An odious fen is there, a dull, dark pool.
And Styx, nine times infolded hems them round.
Yet even the inmost house of death and hell
Listened in wonder, and th' Eumenides
With serpent-wreathed hair. Fell Cerberus
Held his three mouths agape. The windy wheel
That tortures lost Ixion ceased to roll.
Now homeward turning, Orpheus had escaped
These perils manifold; Eurydice,
His own once more, was climbing back to life.
But following far behind her spouse, for so
Proserpina had said. But, ere he knew,
A sudden madness seized the lover's mind —
A fault to be forgiven, could hell forgive.
For when the first clear sunbeam smote her brow,
He, heedless, ah! and his resolves undone,
Paused, looking backward on Eurydice.
Then all his work was nothing, for the law
Of death's grim king was broken. Then three times
Loud thunders o'er Avernus' waters rolled.

'Orpheus,' she cried, ' what madness this, that slays
My wretched self and thee ? Oh, once again
They call me back, the unrelenting powers.
Sleep falls upon my fading sight. Farewell!
Deep night is round me and I drift away,
No longer thine, alas! but lifting thee
My helpless hands.'

             She spake and suddenly
Sank from his sight, like cloudy smoke that fades
And flies away mingling with viewless air.
He stood, a shadow grasping, and would fain
Speak to her o'er and o'er; but after this
She saw him not. The Stygian boatman gave
No second passage o'er his barrier stream.

What could he more attempt, or whither flee,
Of such a bride twice robbed ? What bitter cry
Can reach the realm of death, or mournful voice
Move the infernal powers? What was she now
But shadow cold, on Stygian shallop borne ?
So he, while seven whole months went by, they say,
Beneath the windy crags and by the shores
Of solitary Strymon weeping strayed.
To caverns cold his sorrows numbering o'er
In music that made tigers tame and lured
The rugged oaks to follow.
                Even so
In poplar shades the mournful nightingale
Her stolen brood bewails, which cruel hands
Have found, and pulled all naked from her nest.
The livelong night she cries, and on one bough
Renews the doleful story, far and wide
Filling the forest with complaint and woe.

His heart could love no more; no spousals new
His purpose changed. In solitude he roved
Far north through frozen fields and Scythian snows,
O'er mountain steeps that wear perpetual cold.
Lamenting loud his lost Eurydice
And Pluto's favors vain. His faithful grief
Angered those Thracian maids whose kiss he scorned.
As madly through Cithaeron's echoing vales
Their bacchanalian, midnight revel sped.
When they had torn the lover limb from limb
And hurled him piecemeal o'er the fields, even then
As Hebrus' rolling current swept along
His head, from white neck rent away, its voice.
Its death-cold tongue, cried forth 'Eurydice!'
The parting breath sighed 'Poor Eurydice !'
'Eurydice! ' the sounding shores replied."

Thus Proteus' tale had end; and with a leap
He plunged him in the sea and where he plunged
Tossed up the wave-crest into whirling foam.
Not so Cyrene, she before he asked,
Unto her trembling son this counsel gave:
" Now may thy heart, dear son, put by its pain.
The plague had this one cause: it was the nymphs
With whom in lofty groves she tripped along.
That sent thy swarms of bees such hapless end.
Go offer gifts. Uplift the suppliant hand
And pray the gentle wood-nymphs to forgive.
Soon will they pardon and thine offering heed,
Letting their anger die. But in what form
To make petition, I will first unroll.
Four noble bulls surpassing large and strong
Who now are pastured on the uplands green
Of this Lycaean hill, these shalt thou choose;
And with them take as many heifers fair

Whose necks no yoke has touched. Build then
Four altars at the wood-nymphs' favored shrine
And let the sacred streams of blood run down
From throats of victims slain; but leave behind
Their lifeless bodies in the leafy grove.
When after these things the ninth morn is come.
Pay funeral sacrifice in Orpheus' name
And with oblivion's poppies garland o'er,
Slaying a black-fleeced sheep. Then to the grove
Return, and to th' appeased Eurydice
Make thankful offering of a heifer slain."

No tarrying now ! But straightway he fulfilled
His mother's words. He sought the favored shrine
And raised the wood-nymphs the four altars due.
Four noble bulls surpassing large and strong,
Four unyoked heifers brought he; afterward
When the ninth morn had risen, then he paid
The sacrifice to Orpheus, and retraced
His footsteps to the grove. There suddenly
Men saw a wonder passing strange: the sides
Of the slain cattle, now turned soft, buzzed loud
With swarming bees; the belly and the ribs
Were teeming; and the bees in formless clouds
Streamed upward to a tree-top, and hung down
In pointed cluster from the swinging bough.

Thus have I made my songs of well-kept farms,
Of flocks withal and trees, while Caesar's power
Was launching the vast thunder of his war
Over the deep Euphrates, publishing
By conquest his supreme and just decrees
Unto the grateful nations, taking so
His pathway to the gods. The selfsame days
I, Virgil, passed in sweet Parthenope,

Busied and blest in unrenowned repose,
I that erewhile, when youthful blood was bold
Played with the shepherd's muse, and made my song
Of Tityrus beneath the beech-tree's shade.

CHAPTER V

SELECTED HONEY RECIPES
FROM APICIUS

DE RE COQUINARIA

MULSUM

Roman honeyed wine, often (and wrongly) translated as mead.

To make excellent honeyed wine: take straightway the once-pressed must from the wine vat, meaning the must that has flowed from the grapes before they have been greatly trodden.

Make it with grapes from vines which grow upon trees and that were picked on a dry day.

Put ten pounds *(7.25 lbs / 3.29 kg)* of the best honey into an urn *(3.46 gallons (US) / 13.1 liters)* of must and, after neatly mixing them together, fill a jug and immediately seal it with plaster and place it on a floor.

After 31 days, you will have to open the jug and strain the must into another vessel that you'll plaster up and place it where smoke will reach it.

WONDERFUL SPICED WINE

Pour intro a brass vase 2 sextarii *(38.5 ounces / 1086ml)* of wine and 15 parts of honey.

Heat on a slow wood fire, constantly stirring the mixture with a spatula.

When the liquid starts boiling, add some dashes of wine drop by drop unless you prefer to stop the boiling by taking the mixture out of the fire.

When the mixture has cooled down, make it boil again.

Repeat this a second time, and then a third.

Remove from the fire and let it rest till the next day.

The next day, skim the mixture.

Add 4 ounces *(110g)* of pepper, 3 scruples *(0.12oz / 3.42g)* of grounded mastic, 1 drachm *(3g)* of nard, 1 drachm *(3g)* of saffron, 5 dried dates that have been pitted and crushed after macerating in wine.

Once done, pour 18 sextarii *(346oz / 9774ml)* of sweet wine. Boil the mixture.

SPICED HONEY WINE

This unalterable honey wine is given to wayfarers.

In a small barrel pour skimmed honey mixed with ground pepper.

At the moment of drinking, mix the honey with the wine. It is recommended to pour some wine into the honey mixture *(melizomum)* to facilitate it's flow.

OF IMPROVING A SPOILED HONEY

You can turn honey into a saleable product by mixing one part of spoiled honey with two parts of good honey.

OF IDENTIFYING A SPOILED HONEY

Immerse a branch of elecampane in honey and light it. If the honey ignites, it is not spoiled.

OXYPORON

Oxyporon was used to improve or activate digestion.

2 oz. of cumin
1 oz. of ginger
1 oz. of green rue
6 scruples *(0.24oz. / 6.84g)* of salt peter
12 scruples *(0.48oz. / 13.68g)* of plump dates,
1 oz. of pepper
9 oz. of honey.
Macerate in vinegar the Ethiopian, Syrian or Libyan cumin.
Drain and grind the cumin with the other ingredients.
Thicken by adding the honey, and add some vinegar garum if necessary.

ROAST SUCKLING PIG WITH HONEY AND MILK (PORCELLUM ASSUM TRACTOMELITUS)

Clean the piglet, empty by the throat, and dry.
Crush 1 ounce *(27.4g)* of pepper, honey and wine. Put, heat, break dry dough and mix the pieces in the earthen pot. Stir with a twig of green laurel and cook until smooth and thickened.
Fill the pig with the stuffing, tighten, wrap in parchment paper, put in the oven, dress and serve.

SALTED FISH & CHEESE DISH

Take any kind of salted fish. Cook in oil and remove the bones.

Take pieces of cooked brains, the fish meat, minced chicken livers, boiled eggs and boiled soft cheese.

Heat all this in a dish. Grind pepper, lovage, oregano, rue *(ruta graveolens)* seeds with wine, honeyed wine *(mulsum)* and oil.

Cook everything on a slow fire. Bind the sauce with raw eggs.

Arrange the dish properly and sprinkle with small cumin seeds and serve.

FOR GAME BIRD ROASTS

Pepper, lovage, coriander, caraway, dry onion, mint, egg yolks, dates, honey, vinegar, garum, oil and wine.

SWEET CAKE

Take fine wheat flour, cook in hot water and make a very hard porridge of it.

Thereupon spread on a pan, and cut like sweets when cool.

Fry in the best oil, take them out, pour honey, sprinkle with pepper and serve.

They will be better if prepared with milk instead of water.

SWEET CAKE II

Crush pepper, pine nuts, honey, rue and raisin wine with milk. Work well with dough, cook covered with some eggs, pour honey and serve.

SWEET CAKE III

Remove the crust from fine wheat bread, break in rather big bite size pieces, soak in milk, and fry in oil.

Cover with honey and serve.

Made in the USA
Columbia, SC
19 September 2024

42664256R00057